Old Story Time

Trevor Rhone

Caribbean students' edition prepared by
Mervyn Morris

Harold Jaghai

PEARSON
Longman

PEARSON EDUCATION LIMITED

Edinburgh Gate
Harlow
Essex CM20 2JE
England
and Associated Companies throughout the World

www.pearsoncaribbean.com

© Pearson Education Limited 2010

Old Story Time was first published in 1981 by Longman
Old Story Time and *Smile Orange* was first published in Longman
Caribbean Writers series 1987
This edition is based on the text published by Longman in 1987

This edition published in 2010 by Pearson Education Limited
Copyright in the notes © 2010, Pearson Education Limited
978-1-4082-4514-9

10 9 8 7 6 5
12 11 10
Printed and bound in Great Britain by Clays Ltd, Bungay, Suffolk

Contents

Using the student edition

To the student

To help you to prepare for your exam, the student edition of
Old Story Time includes:

- the complete play
- notes to point out important themes and features
- activities to help you to understand key points and themes
- outlines of the plot with questions
- background information about Trevor Rhone, Jamaican
  Theatre, and the key issues of the play
- a *CSEC*-style exam paper

To the teacher

CSEC Student Editions are designed to meet the varied and
complex needs of students working throughout the 11–16
age-range.

The notes

These have been designed to meet the requirements of the new
English B syllabus, covering themes, values, characterisation,
and the playwright's craft. Particular attention has been paid to
the elements that make drama unique as a literary genre, which
is a key skill the examiners will assess in the final exam. Such
elements include:

> Performance
> Stage Directions
> Character
> The effect of stagecraft (e.g. lighting, props, set design)
> on the development of themes and characterisation

The notes should not be substituted for careful study of the
play itself. Students should be encouraged to read and re-read
scenes, act them out, and if possible, to see a performance for
themselves.

Plot summaries

This section, which directs attention to important detail in the plot, can be used for revision and testing. Questions follow each summary to provoke discussion and analysis of events so far. These could be used in class, or for homework.

Activities

Activities can be found within the notes to encourage students to explore new ideas. These are suitable for use in the classroom.

Questions

The **Questions about the play** at the end of the notes are suitable for homework, classwork, and revision, and relate to themes and ideas found throughout the play.

The **Exam-practice questions** are written in the style of the questions that students will answer in their *CSEC* examination, and suggested mark schemes are provided. This section is suitable for use as a practice examination paper.

Trevor Rhone

Trevor Rhone (1940-2009) was born in Jamaica into a large black family – twenty-three[1] children in all. He grew up in Bellas Gate, a village in rural St Catherine. As a little boy he attended what Jamaicans call 'tea meetings', concerts at which members of the audience offer to pay small sums to take a performer off or to put the performer back on stage. 'Before I had seen a play,' he said, 'I knew pretty much what my life's work should be.'[2] At the age of nine he had decided: he was going to be an actor. He attended primary schools in St Catherine and had his secondary education (1952-57) at Beckford and Smith's (now St Jago High School) in Spanish Town. He became involved in the Secondary Schools' Drama Festival and, later, in the annual Little Theatre Movement pantomime. After leaving school he took various jobs and began to write radio plays. At a time when he had been thinking seriously of going abroad to study, he happened to meet the Trinidadian actor Edric Connor who suggested the Rose Bruford College in Kent, England, but also cautioned, 'Whatever they teach you, forget half of it.'[3]

At Rose Bruford (1960-63) Rhone learnt a great deal about the history and development of theatre, stagecraft, and how to make optimum use of slender resources; about mime, the use of the body, the voice; and so on. His one important reservation about the experience was that he was being forced, in that ambience, to deny his own roots and to acknowledge the roots of England instead. 'That, I think, was the real hazard of the place: that they tried to make you into somebody that you were not, and make you into what *they* were.'[4]

He returned to Jamaica and took a job as a teacher, for which Rose Bruford had also trained him. But he was distressed at the low salary and the fact that little seemed to be happening in theatre. He found the climate 'desert-like.'[5] After nine months he travelled to England again. But in London he was unhappy with the type of role available to the black actor; so he went back to Jamaica in 1965. This time he and seven associates decided that they would make something happen. They called themselves *Theatre '77*, their mission being to establish professional theatre in Jamaica within twelve years. The beginnings were difficult. For one reason or another,[6] many of the original people fell away. Two of those who stuck it out were Trevor Rhone and Yvonne Jones (later Yvonne Brewster). Rehearsals took place on the verandah at the home of Yvonne's parents, the Clarkes, until (according to *Bellas Gate Boy*) a message from Mr Clarke dispatched them to the garage.[7] After a while the enthusiasts were allowed to clear junk from the garage and, phase by phase, to convert it into the Barn Theatre, seating 150 people.

In the early years of the Barn Theatre Rhone taught at more than one school. Wishing to produce a pantomime for one of them, St Andrew Technical, he found that the English scripts available did not fully engage the interest of his students; and, encouraged by the headmaster, he took time off from classes to write a Jamaican *Cinderella*. The show went well, and next year Mr Rhone was expected to produce another pantomime. A year later he produced a third. In 1969, fearing he might end up 'a frustrated old man',[8] he decided to resign from teaching and attempt to write full-time.

He wrote at least seventeen plays. He also wrote film scripts, including *Smile Orange* (a version of his first big theatre hit), *Milk and Honey, One Love* and (with Perry Henzell) *The Harder They Come*. His published plays include *Smile Orange, School's Out, Old Story Time, Two Can Play* and the autobiographical monologue *Bellas Gate Boy*.

In her book on West Indian theatre Judy Stone writes of Trevor Rhone: 'He is a rare breed, the serious writer with the common touch. His gift for comedy gives his works mass appeal, and makes palatable, easily digestible, and memorable, his forthright indictments of the racism, bigotry, opportunism, corruption, idleness, and other unlovely traits that make his own Jamaican people, and by extension the human race, less than he believes they might be.'[9]

1 He used to say twenty-one. But see *Bellas Gate Boy* (Oxford: Macmillan Caribbean, 2008), p. 4.

2 Interview, *Jamaica Journal (JJ)* Vol. 16 No. 1, February 1983, p.3. See also Mervyn Morris, *Making West Indian Literature* (Kingston: Ian Randle Publishers, 2005), p. 66.

3 *JJ* p. 4; *Making* p. 66.

4 *JJ* p. 4; *Making* p. 67.

5 *JJ* p. 4; *Making* p. 67.

6 For some of the reasons, see *Bellas Gate Boy* pp. 29-32.

7 *Bellas Gate Boy* p. 32.

8 *Bellas Gate Boy* p. 40.

9 Judy S.J. Stone, *Studies in West Indian Literature: Theatre* (London: Macmillan Caribbean, 1994), p. 40.

Glossary

buck	stub (one's toe)
drudge	wear (shoes) habitually
hex	curse
jeysey ears	filthy person (literally, a person with dirty ears)
primp	preen oneself; show off
quabs	friends
quattie	penny, ha 'penny
toto	small round brown cake (made of flour and brown sugar)
wutliss	worthless

Old Story Time

First performed in Nassau at the Dundas Centre for the Performing Arts by the Bahamas Drama Circle on 19 April 1979 with the following cast:

PA BEN	Winston Saunders
GEORGE	John Trainer
MAMA (MISS AGGY)	Pandora Gomez
LEN	Calvin Cooper
LOIS	Gwen Kelly
PEARL	Joan Vanderpool

Directed by:	Trevor D. Rhone

The Setting

Three frames and some very basic wooden furniture against a black back-drop and black wing flats make up the simple setting. Up Right two frames joined together, one angled Down Right, and the other running toward Up Right Centre, suggest the exterior-interior of MAMA's house, and later the interior of LEN's house. A sliding door, not in use when the area is used as MAMA's house, fits into the frame angled Down Right. A picture of Jesus hangs on the wall. During 'Change the house round', the picture is reversed to reveal LEN's college diploma. Reversible panels hang on either side of the door. For MAMA's house they are painted to suggest peeling wattle-and-daub walls; for LEN's house they are painted to suggest a marble finish.

Supports and cross-pieces serve as shelves on the frame running toward Up Right Centre. An old curtain hung in the centre of the frame reflects MAMA's poverty. The curtain is removed during 'Change the house round' to reveal books, candle-holders, a vase, etc.

The third frame Down Left suggests PA BEN's old house. It stands on a six-inch raised level which serves as his verandah. A practical window in two halves opens out towards the audience. The open door is cut into the frame. This area remains constant throughout.

The area in front of the stage – that is, between the stage and the first row of chairs (normally reserved for the orchestra pit) – serves as part of the playing area.

Furniture

MAMA'S HOUSE

(i)   An old bureau

(ii) A low bench

PA BEN'S AREA

(i)   Two old wooden chairs on his verandah

(ii) A piece of furniture Up Left that serves as storage for his tobacco, etc.

LEN'S HOUSE/GEORGE'S OFFICE IN THE BANK. The areas are freely interchangeable.

(i)   A coffee table

(ii) Four wooden chairs; three serve as a sofa Centre Stage behind the coffee table.

(iii) A small table and the fourth wooden chair serve as the office furniture in GEORGE's bank, and as part of LEN's living area.

(iv) The piece of furniture Up Left and the wooden stool serve as a bar in LEN's house.

With proper design and construction, the same piece of furniture serves as the bureau in MAMA's house, as well as the table in LEN's house/the Bank. Also, the coffee table covered with matting serves as the low bench in MAMA's house.

Costumes

Thorough research will help in the accuracy of the designs. It is important to reflect the dress styles of the past.

I suggest a simple device to help the flashbacks in the play, which is the use of red-coloured accessories, e.g. when MAMA (Miss Aggy) in Act I re-enacts the scene in which Mr Mac encouraged her to buy a house for her son, she replaces her black hat with a red one, removing it at the end of the sequence.

LEN, as a boy, dresses in the style of thirty-odd years ago. As an adult he dresses in the mode of the successful banker in today's world. A red school cap helps the transition in Act Two – Scene One.

PA BEN: Old baggy pants, a time-worn shirt, along with an old-fashioned jacket. An old felt hat completes him.

PEARL, as a teenager, dresses in the style of thirty-odd years ago. Her clothes are well worn, however.

As pregnant PEARL, in her early twenties, her dress is even more tattered.

As old PEARL, she is literally dressed in rags. Though only in her forties, she looks much older.

THE REAL ESTATE DEVELOPER: smart and modern.

MARGARET: dresses expensively in the style of thirty-odd years ago, and, most importantly, a flowing hairpiece.

LOIS: expensively modern.

MAMA: market-lady attire, head-tie, apron, old shoes, etc. Her torn clothes are simply cut from inexpensive material.

GEORGE: expensive-looking suits, ties, etc.

When the actors sit round PA BEN as the villagers, they wear street clothes that facilitate quick changes to the roles they will play, e.g. the actress playing MAMA needs only to add an apron to become the market lady.

All the characters are black except GEORGE, a high brown man, and MARGARET, a fair-skinned girl. The same actress plays PEARL, the REAL ESTATE DEVELOPER and MARGARET. Ideally, a fair-skinned girl should play the part (it is easier to make her look black than to make a black girl look fair-skinned).

Week 1/4

The group on stage go off by jumping sideways with feet together as if in a children's game.

Act One

Len is taken from a boy to a man widespread discrimination on the grounds of colour

Scene One

1. lighting (as an essential production element)

[*The stage and auditorium go to black. In the darkness we hear the actors singing a quiet, lyrical folk song. Very soon we see the glow of PA BEN's lantern.*]

PA BEN: [*Over the song, sings*] Old Story Time. Old Story Time.

[*As he enters the auditorium, the lights come up fully on him.*]

He is addressing the audience as well metaphor

The audience may respond here as well

[*Speaks*] Evening, one and all. Everybody hearty? What happen, you people mouth join church or what? You don't have voice to answer me? Everybody hearty? [*The actors respond 'Yes, Pa Ben'.*] That's better. [*To the audience*] Make yourselves comfortable on them nice chairs. You people lucky, years ago when A was a boy and A use to go to listen to story, it was never in no fancy place like this, with all them pretty fandangles, pretty lights and whatnot. No, sir.

[*The actors in the play start appearing from various directions and start moving to the Storyteller's area, where they will become PA BEN's immediate audience.*]

On an evening in the district, we would gather at the village square, everybody gather round the shop piazza, some sit 'pon old drum, others 'pon the old crocus bags filled with salt, everybody chatting, some meddling in people's business, others giving remembrance to who dead the week before, who saw the ghost and what not, and my father was the chief Storyteller when him feel in the mood. [*PA BEN leaves the auditorium and goes up to his storytelling area.*] But A tell you, give him a bottle of whites, an' two twos him was slap bang in the mood. He hem.

VILLAGES/ACTORS: Him clear him throat.

PA BEN: And that was the signal to launch into a story. Who present would run go call the rest.

ACTRESS WHO   [*Running to call off*] Pa Ben ready! Run come!
WILL PLAY LOIS: Story time!

PA BEN: An' mi father would wax warm, him mind 'pon the story an' one eye 'pon the young gal them.

6

Ah boy, those were the days. Yes, A can still hear the bamboo clarinet, and the fife a whistle, and the drum a lick, an' A can still see miself dress up in all mi finery stepping into the dance yard. *[He re-enacts the memory.]* And in those days they had a new fancy dance called the 'corkscrew', and A was the champion corkscrewer. *[He dances, much to the delight of his audience who tease him, 'Watch your back, Pa Ben, careful, Pa Ben,' etc.]* If any of you young gals here don't believe me, then meet me when the story done! Yes, those were the days. Good times and bad times, no opportunity for us black people, no water, no road, no 'lectric light. Sweet-mouth politician promise to bring down the moon, cut it up and hang it 'pon stick so we could read bible when night come. Ah boy, sixty years later, they don't even cut the stick yet. Ah well, that is another story.

Christianity

ACTOR WHO WILL PLAY GEORGE: So how you use to read?

PA BEN: With mi bottle lamp. And in war days when oil short, A catch two firefly, put them in a bottle, light up the place same way. Ah boy, war days, no flour, no saltfish, no soap, the shops empty, but that too is another story.

exaggerates about the fireflies

ACTRESS WHO WILL PLAY PEARL: Howdy, Pa Ben. *[As she comes on.]*

PA BEN: All well. All well. Come sit down. A ready for you. Open this for me. *[Giving her his bottle of white rum.]* The tongue nuh fully oil yet, but A going to begin. *[PEARL returns the opened bottle to PA BEN. He takes a big swig, to more comments from his audience, 'Mind you rotten out yuh liver', 'Him don't have no liver', etc. The over one hundred per cent proof rum makes him temporarily lose his voice but he quickly recovers. He signals to the actress who will play MAMA. They whisper momentarily and she goes off.]* A did live in a certain big yard, next door to some a the people who the story concern, so you see A have first-hand knowledge. What A don't know as a fact, A will make up as A go along, and if A can't do it by miself, mi friend here will help me.

exaggeration

This song serves to emphasized, by contrast, our engagement in an old story time.

children's songs

	[*Indicating his rum bottle.*] Now how the tune go again?
ACTRESS WHO WILL PLAY PEARL:	Me know, me know. [*She jumps up and immediately starts to sing a very uptempo blues version of the folk song, with much body gyration.*]
	Once upon a time
	There was a merry ol' time
	The monkey chew tobacco
	And he spit white lime.

[*The actors/villagers listen to the version of the song, bemused.*]

PA BEN:	That is not the tune.
ACTOR WHO WILL PLAY GEORGE:	No, but it sound nice. [*They all join in.*]
	The bull frog jump from bank to bank … [*They start going off.*]
PA BEN:	An' he never touch water. [*He chants.*] Ol' Story Time. Ol' Story Time. [*As he goes into his house.*]

✓ 2 a.

[*The lights come up on the rest of the stage as* MAMA, *endearingly called Miss Aggy by* PA BEN *and Miss G by the others, enters, dressed in her market wear. A basket sits on top of her head; she carries another in her hand. She looks tired as if at the end of a long journey. She comes on, sets her baskets down on the bench, then calls …*]

MAMA:	Len! [*pause.*] Don't tell me him not here. Lennie! [*pause.*] Watch me an' him today. Lennard! After I tell him to stay in the house an' study him book [*She starts looking around the yard for him.*], him make me come back an ' don't find him in the yard. [*She calls out once more.*] Lennard! [*Pause.*] Lennard! Pa Ben, Pa Ben! [*She calls across the yard.*]
PA BEN:	Oi.
MAMA:	You see Lennard?
PA BEN:	A think him went to market wid you.
MAMA:	No. A left him here to study him book.
PA BEN:	Him about. So how was the market?
MAMA:	Couldn't be worse this week. A had to give away half of the things, jus' so A never had to carry them back. An' like a bad luck, the damn jackass foot go lame up on me, an' me had to trot the ten mile come home.
PA BEN:	Lawd.
MAMA:	What to do? Anyway, A bring something for you.
PA BEN:	Is what?

She brings a gift for her friend

MAMA: Wait, nuh. *[She digs into her basket. He cleans his hands in his clothes in anticipation. She hands him a big hymn book.]*

Christianity

PA BEN: For me? Thank you. *[He opens the book.]* Nice print. *[A hymn catches his eye and he sings.* 'Rock of ages cleft for me ...'

today is Saturday

Christianity

MAMA: So you going to service tomorrow?

PA BEN: A not to make up mi mind yet. *[He goes into his little house.]*

He's avoiding the commitment

MAMA: Is fourth Sunday, so Reverend Greaves should come up.

PA BEN: Then I have to try an' go.

MAMA: *[As she watches him go off]* Try. Old devil! A going down the road to look see if A see the one Lennard. *[She takes the market basket offstage.]*

He's actually far from being a "Devil"

PA BEN: *[He opens his window and looks out at her.]* Buy penny oil, hapenny salt, an' quattie bread for me. See the money here. *[Taking out a handkerchief. The money is securely knotted in it.]*

MAMA: All right. Where A leave the switch? *[As she hunts around for it.]*

PA BEN: Nuh worry beat him.

MAMA: If him can't hear him mus' feel. *[As she is going off]* Is you help spoil him.

PA BEN: Lawd! Harass the poor boy so!

MAMA: *[As she is leaving she sees a switch on the lower level.]* Ah, see it here. Wait till A catch up with him, A going to scour his behind for him this evening.

PA BEN: *[Speaking directly to the audience]* If A had mi wits about me, A would save the boy a licking that evening. A should tell him mother that is me send him out. A have to find him before she catch up with him. Lennie! *[As he goes off calling.* MAMA *can also be heard calling offstage,* 'Lennard!'*]*

b. *[LEN chases PEARL on from Up Left. He catches up with her and touches her on her bosom.]*

Len's longing for a normal childhood; the village temptations to early sexual activity

LEN: Touch. *[Both laughing like mad.]* Okay, your time.

PEARL: All right.

LEN: Come on then. *[He presents his pelvic area for her to touch.]*

PEARL: *[Feigns at touching, then suddenly lunges at him.]*Touch!

LEN: You never touch.

Pearl – name of a contraceptive

PEARL:	Touch.
LEN:	I finish play.
PEARL:	You have to go home?
LEN:	No.
PEARL:	Yuh mother must be soon come from market.
LEN:	So?
PEARL:	I know what will happen if she come home and don't find you.
LEN:	She can't do me nutten.
PEARL:	Except tie you to the bed-head and murder you.
LEN:	Tie who?
PEARL:	You same one. Go on like you is a big man.
LEN:	Big man, yes.
PEARL:	In yuh pants.
LEN:	You want to see it? *[He chases her threateningly.]*
PEARL:	You too rude. Play bad when yuh mother not around. Is only because she gone to market why you manage to t'ief out.
LEN:	I don't have to t'ief out.
PEARL:	So you say, but everybody notice how since you get to go to the high school, how she strict with you more than ever, like she don't want you to mash ants. You mus' just primps. Is like you turning into a real high posh. Hoititoity. All drudge shoes!
LEN:	You see me have on shoes?
PEARL:	You hide them up the road man; when is time to go home, you put them on. Go home.
LEN:	I go home when I ready.
PEARL:	All right. Come we go down by the river. *[As she walks and stands directly in front of him. Their bodies are very close. They are both laughing.]*
LEN:	So come we go.
PEARL:	A don't want yuh mother to beat you, you know. *[As she pushes herself even closer to him.]*
LEN:	Last one reach is a dead dog! *[They race off, then freeze on the spot. When they break the freeze they are in the river, playing away, commenting on how cold the water is, accusing each other of wetting each other's hair, etc. MAMA appears behind them.]*
MAMA:	Jesus Saviour, pilot me. *[The playing ceases immediately. PEARL scampers off. LEN attempts to run away.]* Don't bother to run. If you run A murder you tonight. Come here. *[He comes slowly and*

Handwritten margin notes:

primp – preen oneself; show off

drudge – wear (shoes) habitually

In contrast to her Christian-like nature; she should not be compelled to "murder" Len

10

	tentatively towards her. She grabs him.] Don't A tell you not to leave the house? Don't A tell you to stay in the house an' study yuh books?
LEN:	A was studying all morning, Mama. A just came out for a little breeze.
MAMA:	Well then, feel the breeze! *[As she beats him]* Don't A tell you … Don't mix up … Don't carouse. Who is di gal?
LEN:	Is Miss Esmeralda daughter, Pearl, Mama.
MAMA:	Pearl? An' what you is to she?
LEN:	She is mi friend, Mama.
MAMA:	Miss Esmeralda frowsy-tail, jiggerfoot, jeysey-ears, board head gal is your friend? Where is yuh ambition? You don't have any ambition? After A struggle out mi soul case to send you to big shot high school, you come home come mix up with that little dry-head gal? How much time A must tell you, don't mix up with the little dutty black gal dem in the district? How much time A must tell you, anything black nuh good? She is no advancement. It look like A will have to beat it into you. *[She drags him up.]* A will hang you, you know. Them little dry-head gal will drag you down! *[As she pushes him to the ground again.]* You think A want to treat you like this? A only want what is best for you. Trust Mama. Mama knows best. Leave out the dutty black gal them, concentrate on yuh books, for life is hard when you black, but with a little education you still have a chance. When time come for you to have girlfriend, A have a nice girl pick out for you. Miss Margaret, Reverend Greaves daughter, a nice brown girl with tall hair down to her back. She is advancement, you hear me. *[She picks him up.]*
LEN:	Yes, Mama.

[MAMA shoves him off home. As they are going she continues]

MAMA:	Miss Margaret. You hear what A tell you? Miss Margaret. Miss Margaret.
LEN:	Yes, Mama. *[As she hits him a series of blows going off.]*
PA BEN:	*[Coming on to his area.]* Miss Margaret. Miss Margaret. That's all could ring in the boy's ears, year after year. Miss Margaret. Like a drum. *[He*

she sees the importance of education.

Mama is prejudice against her own race (Pearl).

she believes this & wants Len to accept it too

Mama's love for Len. Tough love.

1.1

Pa Ben is reminding
us that as a
storyteller. he can
withhold information
until he is ready to
release it.

friendship between
Pa Ben & Len

she would not have
approved of his Black
girlfriend.
Pa Ben hates malice

b.

comes directly down to the audience.] You have to understand Miss Aggy. She wouldn't even have a black chicken in her yard. One chop, off with the head. Miss Margaret was like an obsession with her. The years went by, and the boy study him books, day and night, an' him pass all him exams with flying colours, yet still him couldn't get a job in the bank. But later for that. One day A happen to be in a next district about three miles from here, and A happen to see the boy with a pretty black girl. We two eyes make four, an' him beg me not to say anything to him mother, and A kept him secret. In fact, A became him confederate, carry message, arrange meeting, dat sort a thing, till one day the boy announce say him get scholarship to go to foreign to further him studies. Three or four weeks after him leave the pretty black girl send to call me, Miss Lois was her name, an' she give me a letter from Missa Lenny, telling me thanks for everything. One thing him beg me. Don't tell him mother say A hear from him. It was a hard secret to keep, but A couldn't bruck it. As the months went by Miss Aggy still got no proper word from the boy. She worry till she all take in sick. *[MAMA enters through the door Up Right looking sick and forlorn: She sits on the low bench with her back to the audience.]* But still A had to hold mi tongue. Why was he carrying feelings for her? All A could do was to try and comfort her.

[He leaves the lower area and goes towards his house, calling out to her.]

Miss Aggy!

MAMA: How you do, Pa Ben?

PA BEN: All well. All well. *[He continues into his house to get a basket of peas and returns almost immediately.]* How is the feeling an' you?

MAMA: So so, thank God. *[She leaves her area and comes over to him.]*

PA BEN: You went back to the doctor? *[He sits on a chair beside his little house and starts to shell the peas.]*

MAMA: Waste mi money an' go. Him say is all in mi mind.

PA BEN: Worrination. Yes, is a bad sickness. Stop fret yuhself. Missa Lenny soon write.

Act 1 Scene 1

MAMA:	A convince more an' more say something bad happen to him. *[She sits on a stool beside him and starts to help him shell the peas.]*
PA BEN:	No. Nutten nuh happen. Me sure a dat.
MAMA:	How you so sure?
PA BEN:	Me just sure.
MAMA:	Den why him nuh write? Is over a year now since him gone, an' all A get is one postcard say him reach. Lawd a mercy!
PA BEN:	Nuh cry.
MAMA:	A worry, A fret, A pray.
PA BEN:	Is all right.
MAMA:	Mass Len wouldn't neglect me so. Him know I would be worried. All sorts of things going through mi head. A wonder if him dead?
PA BEN:	Nuh think dat.
MAMA:	The only other thing left to think is that. Lawd!
PA BEN:	What now?
MAMA:	Say that somebody in the district burn a candle on his head.
PA BEN:	Miss G, shame on you! Who in the district would do a thing like that? *[He goes to the little storage area by his house to look for his tobacco.]*
MAMA:	Plenty a them right here, smile up with me to mi face, but in they heart they malice me off, jealous say mi son doing too well. Me nuh forget the time when him did win the scholarship to the high school. Now him get scholarship again gone to University, they will do anything to bring me down. Me nuh trus' them.
PA BEN:	You suspect anybody in particular?
MAMA:	Everybody. Them will do it.
PA BEN:	Me too?
MAMA:	Excep' you.

[The girl PEARL whom we saw as LEN's playmate goes by the house. She is now no longer young and lively, but a broken-down shell of her old self, pregnant, and very laden down. She crosses the stage on the lower level during her conversation with MAMA.]

PEARL:	Howdy, Miss G.
MAMA:	Is who that now?
PA BEN:	A don't catch the voice.
PEARL:	Howdy, Pa Ben.

Handwritten margin notes: Lying to her; deceptive to her — christianity — Being negative — Obeah — Being negative. Making assumptions.

13

rumour between Mama & Pa Ben about Pearl

PA BEN: All well. All well.

PEARL: How the feeling an' you, ma'am?

MAMA: Bearing up.

PEARL: *[Stopping to ask]* An' how Missa Lenny when you hear?

She lies

MAMA: Oh, couldn't be better. Got a letter from him only last week. Doing well with him lessons. Say to tell everybody howdy.

PEARL: Thank him, Ma'am, an' when you write, say we all proud a him, an' him mus' take care a himself.

MAMA: A will tell him.

PEARL: All right then, Ma'am, me gone again.

rumour

MAMA: Walk good. *[As PEARL goes, PA BEN looks at MAMA in amazement.]* It hurts mi soul case to tell lie, but what else me can do? Me nuh want them to spread it around the district say him dash me 'way. Me just have to keep up the pretence.

PA BEN: Me understan'. Is who the person?

MAMA: Miss Esmeralda daughter. The one they call Pearl.

PA BEN: She? A thought the face look familiar, like somebody me know, but what a way she mash up! Nuh young somebody?

MAMA: Bad life.

PA BEN: Enh?

quabs – friends

MAMA: Batter batter, she batter batter. Me nuh know why she asking me for Mass Len. After them nuh quabs.

PA BEN: She mash up bad. Nuh person the same age as Missa Lenny?

careless sexual activity in the lower class

MAMA: Few months apart. She nuh more than twenty you see her there. So the ol' careless boy them lash her, is so she breed. A five children she have so far, an' it look to me as if she going up again.

PA BEN: Yes, it look to me as if she taking spring. The young girls of today don't know when to lock them leg. *[He rests his hand on MAMA's thigh. She looks at him, then removes it.]*

Mama has different standards in comparison to Pearl

MAMA: When me look on her, an' think say if me never did fight an' struggle with the one Mass Len, all now him would be knocking 'bout the district a turn wutliss like the rest a them.

PA BEN: You put him in the right direction. You finish? *[Taking the basket with the peas.]*

Act 1 Scene 1

1.1

MAMA:	Aye. *[He takes the basket into his house.]* The one thing leave to complete him now is for him to married to the nice brown girl with hair down to her back that me pick out for him.
PA BEN:	*[Opens the window and looks out at her.]* Yuh mind still set on the Reverend daughter, eh?
MAMA:	Is mi dream. What an excitement that would be in the district. Banquet upon banquet. Is then the people in the district would malice me off.
PA BEN:	*[Returns and stands by his open door.]* Missa Lenny did intimate anything about Miss Margaret before him leave?
MAMA:	Me did pry him, but him never say much.
PA BEN:	What him say exactly?
MAMA:	Well, when me pry him, all A could hear him say was, 'Arrr y say Mama'.
PA BEN:	Say what Miss G? *[As he walks towards her.]*
MAMA:	A so me hear, a so me tell you. *[PA BEN repeats it as well.]* I put it down to say him was concentrating so hard on him books. 'Member how him use to lock up all day, all night a study? Most o' the times A didn't want to disturb him, so I would keep mi distance.
PA BEN:	*[Sitting beside her]* I can understand that, but him was a little too withdrawn, too quiet. It wasn't natural.
MAMA:	Come to think of it, I agree with you. Maybe he over-concentrate on him lessons that him mind was like … Pa Ben?
PA BEN:	Yes, Miss Aggy.
MAMA:	A wonder if the books fly up in him head and mad him? Is that!
PA BEN:	Come now, Miss Aggy.
MAMA:	*[Repeats LEN's inarticulateness]* 'Arrr y say Mama'. That nuh the first sign of madness?
PA BEN:	Yuh mind playing tricks on you.
MAMA:	No! Nice quiet dutiful loving boy. *[As she cries.]*
PA BEN:	Think about something else. Don't forget is Pa Zaccy nine night tonight.
MAMA:	Is eight days already?
PA BEN:	Come, we going to sing Sankey tonight. *[He starts singing and dancing.]*

She is avoiding the question

15

Rice an' peas
Rice an' peas
An' coconut oil
Hard dough bread
An' Johnny cake

[He tries to get her involved in the little song till she gives in. They sing for a little while, till she breaks.]

MAMA: A don't feel up to it.

PA BEN: You mus' be forget how Pa Zaccy was cantankerous when he was living, quick to take umbrage at any little slight. Now him dead, him duppy going to be miserable. You better go pay yuh respects an' give him a good send-off. If not, you know him will take up residence on yuh door step an' haunt you for the rest a yuh days. And anyway is a good opportunity to send a message to the boy.

MAMA: Send message with who?

PA BEN: Pa Zaccy. You forget he was a ol time postman. *[PA BEN laughs at his joke.]* As a matter of fact, I better give him a tot to sweeten him up. *[He drops a few drops from his bottle to the ground.]*

MAMA: Lawd, Pa Ben, you too bad! Take bad things make joke. What I would do without you, all the same? Take mi mind off the boy. A going to tie mi head and come.

[She gets up to go into her house.]

PA BEN: Yes, I have to go spruce up and sweeten up miself to.

[He resets the stage, putting the chairs back in place. PEARL is heard calling off.]

PEARL: Miss G?

PA BEN: Come, sweetheart.

PEARL: Postmistress send this for Miss G. *[He takes the letter and examines it. PEARL is curious.]*

PA BEN: Thank you, sweetheart. *[She goes.]* Miss Aggy! Miss Aggy! *[With great excitement.]*

MAMA: *[Off]* Pa Ben, what's all the excitement?

PA BEN: A letter come.

MAMA: From foreign?

PA BEN: Air mail, an' the king picture 'pon the stamp.

MAMA: *[Coming out with great speed and in much flutter]* Mass

16

[handwritten margin note:] Pa Ben tries to comfort Mama when she receives short letters from Len; Pa Ben knows Len is still carrying feelings for her

Pa Ben also advises Mama not to let anyone know Len is avoiding her (to prevent rumours from spreading)

Len! Holy fathers in heaven! Thank you, Jesus! *Christianity*
[She kisses the letter.] You answer mi prayer.

PA BEN: Thank you, brother Zaccy. *[Sprinkling a little of his rum on the ground]* Open it, nuh, Miss G?

MAMA: A too nervous. Open it for me. *[Handing him back the letter]* Woi, woi, woi!

PA BEN: Calm down. Calm down.

MAMA: Say is good news. Is good news? Him hearty? Him 'member me? What him say? Mi heart! *[PA BEN opens letter very gingerly.]* Quick, man!

PA BEN: A coming. Give me a little time. A nervous too, you know. *[He gets it open.]*

MAMA: A can't read it. Read it for me.

PA BEN: But you know mi eyes dark.

MAMA: Tell me what it say.

PA BEN: If A had mi spectacles …

MAMA: Try an' make it out.

PA BEN: All right. Mek A see. *[As he unfolds the letter, a pound note falls out.]* Money!

MAMA: Money?

PA BEN: Him send money.

MAMA: Where him get money sen' for me an' him not working? *[She puts the money away in her bosom.]* What him say?

PA BEN: The right-hand corner up the top say 'At school' an' the date. The lef -hand corner say 'Dear …

MAMA: Mama.

PA BEN: No. 'Mother.'

MAMA: 'Mother?' Go on.

PA BEN: 'I am fine.'

MAMA: Praise the Lord! *Christianity*

PA BEN: 'Hope you are well.'

MAMA: A feel better already.

PA BEN: 'Enclose see pound sign. One. Busy. Len.'

MAMA: Aye. Mi son remember me. Thank you, Jesus. *[She is lost in reverie and joy, till slowly she realises that the letter is finished.]* Dat's all? *[He shows it to her.]* Him don't even ask how you do. For nobody. Him don't tell me not even love. Just 'Len', dry so.

PA BEN: Him busy, as him say, with him books.

MAMA: Yes, is dat. At least him not dead.

PA BEN: An' him send money.

17

obeah

MAMA: The money is no comfort to me. After so long this is all me get. 'I am fine. Hope you are well. Busy. Len'. [*She goes to* PA BEN *and gives him the letter.*] No, Pa Ben, something definitely wrong. Somebody or something turning mi son against me.

PA BEN: No, Miss Aggy. Don't think that.

MAMA: I am convinced of it. Evil forces at work.

PA BEN: Put that thought out yuh head.

obeah

MAMA: Sweet loving boy when him leave Jamaica. Woi! Them light candle 'pon him head. Woi!

[*As she bawls,* PA BEN *becomes aware that* PEARL *is watching.*]

PA BEN: Miss Aggy. [MAMA *looks to see* PEARL *disappearing.*]

MAMA: Lawd a mercy! If the news get out, me done for. Come, we have to buy her silence..

✓ to
5. protect
rumours
from
spreading

[*As they go chasing after* PEARL, MAMA *goes into her bosom for the pound note. Lights go down, then up almost immediately.*]

rumour

PA BEN: So said, so done. It wasn't easy, 'cause the one Pearl was carrying feelings in her heart against Miss Aggy. But A counsel the chile an' she keep her mouth shut. If that news did get out, it would spread like bush fire, an' if somehow people did learn that the boy was in contact with me, then them would say is me obeah him, so that night

the village people
might say Pa Ben
obeah Len since he
writes to him
(spread rumours)

A write to Missa Lenny an' beg him to make the peace with him mother. Him listen to me an' the letters start to come more frequent, an' Miss Aggy start to feel better in herself, the colour come back into her cheeks, and as the years went by, letter come from all over the place, as far as Africa. A nuh little fret we fret for him, for we know say if lion or tiger never eat him raw, the savages in the bush would catch him, cook him up as stew an' devour him. Praises be, him escape. Some photo him send we, native with face paint up an' just one little piece a cloth wrap aroun' them private, but as to the woman them, woi, the whole a them titty out a door, naked as day. Miss Aggy turn her eye, but me look. Me nuh know what me would do with miself if me was to go to all them places. The thought of them eating me! Anyway as luck would have it, Missa Lenny never tarry too long on the dark

[handwritten: Pa Ben understands & sees Mama's motive for putting Len 1st]

continent. Two twos him was back in England, an' we gave thanks for his deliverance, an' there was no further cause for alarm or concern, till one evening …

MAMA:	Woi. Pa Ben?
PA BEN:	Oi.
MAMA:	Come quick.
PA BEN:	What happen? Is what?
MAMA:	*[Holding her belly and bawling]* Woi!
PA BEN:	What happen?
MAMA:	Now A know. Yes, A know.
PA BEN:	Know what?
MAMA:	A know is who obeah mi son.
PA BEN:	Say what?
MAMA:	A have the proof.
PA BEN:	Say what!
MAMA:	See her there *[Handing PA BEN a photograph.]*
PA BEN:	Mass Len, married?
MAMA:	Is the gal in the picture. Is she.
PA BEN:	Miss Lois.
MAMA:	Miss who?
PA BEN:	Ahm …
MAMA:	You know her?
PA BEN:	No, me nuh know her.
MAMA:	Then how come you call her name?
PA BEN:	How me mus' call her name if me nuh know her? What name me call?
MAMA:	You said Miss Lois.
PA BEN:	Miss Lois? No, me said 'Jesus Christ!'
MAMA:	Me could swear you say 'Miss Lois'.
PA BEN:	You must open yuh ears when me talk.
MAMA:	Me nuh care what she name. Me nuh want her beside mi son. *[She tears the photograph in two, throwing the part with LOIS on the floor.]*
PA BEN:	Shame on you, Miss Aggy. Before you happy for the boy, you come with yuh nonsense. *[Picking up the torn photograph.]*
MAMA:	Nonsense. Shut yuh mouth. A know what A talking about. After I drum it into him head that anything black nuh good, I know is no way him could pick up *that* of him own free will. *[Pointing to the torn photograph to PA BEN's hand.]*

[handwritten right margin: Trying to cover his tracks]

[handwritten right margin: in comparison to Lois (a Christ-like figure – forgiving, showing love)]

Even though Pa Ben disagrees with some of Mama's values (in regards to race), he knows that her main concern is Len

PA BEN:	The boy daddy was a black man. Is obeah you did obeah him?
MAMA:	Black was good enough for me. It not good enough for him. There was better for him. *[To herself]* What happen to Miss Margaret?
PA BEN:	The boy make him own choice.
MAMA:	What happen to Miss Margaret? *[She continues bemoaning the loss of Miss Margaret.]*
PA BEN:	Times changing, Miss Aggy. You have to move with the times. Stop living in the past. Any black woman that did marry the boy, you would jump to the same conclusion. You nuh see that don't make nuh sense. You nuh see that is ignorance.
MAMA:	Is who you calling ignorance? Is who? Kirrout! Is my son and it don't concern you, so mind yuh own business and leave mi property.
PA BEN:	You have to face up to the truth.
MAMA:	What more truth I need? Me nuh forget the years when the boy did cut me off!
PA BEN:	Examine yuhself.
MAMA:	Leave mi property!
PA BEN:	Miss Aggy?
MAMA:	Get off!
PA BEN:	What's so wrong if the boy just want to marry somebody who look like him own mother, eh? Put that in yuh pipe an' smoke it! *[He storms out, but storms right back.]* An' before you make yuh next move an' go set evil forces at work to try an' hit back at the chile, consider the one chance you might be wrong, an' when you done consider that, consider the consequences.

[He storms out again.]

MAMA:	*[Pause. Quietly to herself, bewildered]* But I only wanted what was best for him.
PA BEN:	*[Pushing out the windows of his house, he speaks to the audience.]* Is years now I never had occasion to lose mi temper, but she make me so mad.

[MAMA sits with her back to the audience and starts to change her scarf.]

PA BEN:	*[Coming through the door of his little house]* A year go by, and not a word pass between us. One piece a malice she keep up on me. A try to talk to her. *[He walks over to her space.]* Morning, Miss Aggy.

Kirrout – stop it; get out (clear out)

He is still showing love, avoiding malice & offering her advice even though she orders him off her property.

Mama's love for Len

He tries to eradicate malice with love

Pa Ben tries to exemplify love throughout; to him, Mama's colour prejudice is an obstacle to love

Act 1 Scene 1

1.1

[MAMA's *head flashes around only to flash back again. She does not return the greeting.* PA BEN *returns to the audience.*] It hurt mi soul case how she was going on. [MAMA *changes her scarf again.*] After all, she was mi best friend. A had to keep trying, for me is not one to keep up malice. [*He goes across to her space again.*] Evening, Miss Aggy.

His patience wins her over

MAMA: [*Turning very slowly to him*] Evening.

PA BEN: [*He is stopped in his tracks and needs his chair for support.*] A frighten till A almost faint when she answer me, an' is so we start up again till we start exchange two, three words, but never 'bout the marriage or anything to do with Mass Len, but A know she never go to the obeah man to go hit back at the girl. A guess the one chance that she could have been wrong make her stay her hand. Is a terrible thing when you go to the obeah man to seek vengeance, an' it turn roun' an' come back at you, but A know that in her heart of hearts she was still carrying feelings for the chile. The months turn to years, then one day out of the blue …

Mama is still carrying feelings for Lois

[LEN *enters, dressed in a three-piece suit, carrying a small box.*]

LEN: Mama.
PA BEN: Missa Lenny?
LEN: Hello, Sir.
PA BEN: Wo yoi! Miss Aggy, come look. [*To* LEN] Is Missa Lenny?
LEN: Yes, Sir.
PA BEN: Wo yoi! [*As he holds him, kisses him, dances with him.*] You 'member me?
LEN: How could I forget you, Sir?
PA BEN: Nuh worry with nuh 'Sir' business. I is Pa Ben.
LEN: Pa Ben.
MAMA: Pa Ben, what you was calling me for? [*Then she sees her son.*] Lord have mercy [*very quietly*].
LEN: Mama! [*They hug each other tightly.*]
MAMA: Mass Len! [*She cries.*] Mi heart!
LEN: You okay, Mama?
MAMA: Joy, Mass Len. Joy. How you do?
LEN: Fine, Mama.
MAMA: Mi one son.
LEN: How are you, Mama?

6. ✓

Week 2/4

Christianity

MAMA:	Give God thanks to set eyes on you again.
LEN:	You look well, Mama, not a day older.
PA BEN:	Me take care a her, son.
MAMA:	*[good naturedly]* Get out a mi life. *[To LEN]* Son!
LEN:	Mama.
PA BEN:	Then let him go now, nuh, Miss Aggy?
MAMA:	*[good naturedly]* Come out a mi life.
PEARL:	*[entering on the lower level]* Morning, Miss G.
MAMA:	Morning, Miss Pearl. Miss Pearl, look who come!
PEARL:	But stop, is Missa Lenny?
PA BEN:	You nuh have eyes to see!
MAMA:	You 'member Miss Pearl?

[They look at each other for a little while. PEARL, who is again heavily pregnant, looks twice her age. Her foot is bandaged.]

LEN:	How are you?
PEARL:	Me hearty.
LEN:	And the children?
PEARL:	Them hearty too.
LEN:	How many you have now?

12 children total

PEARL:	Is eleven me gone. This one will make the dozen.
PA BEN:	She all have two called Paul.
PEARL:	Me like the name. *[They all laugh, except LEN who laughs a little embarrassedly.]* Well, me on a little haste, so me gone again. Is nice to see you, Mass Len.
LEN:	Take care of yourself.
PEARL:	All right, sir. *[As she is going.]*
MAMA:	Give her something, nuh, Mass Len? *[Calling after her]* Miss Pearl!
LEN:	Here you are, for the baby when it comes. *[PA BEN and MAMA hug each other excitedly.]*
PEARL:	Thank you, sir, the Lord will bless you. *[LEN watches her go.]*

friendship

PA BEN:	Me a run down by the bush, see if A can get a few starapples for you. A don't forget how you did love them when you was a boy.
LEN:	True, sir. I brought something for you as well, sir.
PA BEN:	When A come back, man. Miss Aggy. *[As he points a finger at her.]*
MAMA:	Come we go inside so we can private. *[They go in.]* Mass Len?
LEN:	Yes, Mama.

Act 1 Scene 1

MAMA:	Mass Len, A don't know where to start. *[She starts to cough.]*
LEN:	You have a bad cough, Mama.
MAMA:	Yes, it been worrying me.
LEN:	Maybe you should go see a doctor.
MAMA:	I was waiting till you come.
LEN:	*[Laughs]* I am not that sort of doctor.
MAMA:	What you mean?
LEN:	I am not a medical doctor.
MAMA:	So what kind a doctor you is?
LEN:	Well I, ah, I have a Ph.D.
MAMA:	A wha'?
LEN:	I, ah, am an economist. Banking. I deal with money matters.
MAMA:	Money doctor? Cooyah! What you saying to me? I never know money could sick. Explain yuhself.
LEN:	Another time, Mama.
MAMA:	No. A been boasting off on everybody how mi son graduate as big doctor. Now you making me to understand you can't even cure fresh cold. Don't tell nobody you is not a true true doctor, you know. You hear me.
LEN:	Okay.
MAMA:	What a distress! Then tell me, you wear white coat an' trumpet to sound the money? *[LEN laughs.]* What you laughing for? Is foolishness me ask you?
LEN:	Another time we'll talk about it, okay?
MAMA:	An' me did so glad to see you.
LEN:	Me too. This is yours. *[Giving her the box he brought on.]*
MAMA:	Thank you. *[As she opens it]* Every time you send a parcel for me, excitement in the district. They come down on me like vulture, for what they can get. Lawd, what a pretty frock! Watch me an' them people when I dress off an' go to church. *[She swings the frock in front of her.]* I can just hear them – 'Lawd, Miss G, you look nice. Give me a borrows nuh', yet behind mi back – 'Nuh ol bruck she get from 'merica'. Ol' hypocrites! Leave them to God, after them never help me struggle? Is nuh one or two times A went to bed hungry so you could eat, you know.

A sacrifice she made for her son so he could see a better way of life than she did.

Mama has made sacrifices for Len

1.1 **Act 1 Scene 1**

LEN:	I haven't forgotten, Mama. *[Slight pause.]*
MAMA:	It really nice. You pick it out for Mama?
LEN:	No. Lois did.
MAMA:	Oh! A don't think it going to fit me. *[She tosses it aside, not too carefully.]* We have a lot to talk about Mass Len.
LEN:	Yes, Mama.
MAMA:	Anyway, you just come, but you know what you could help me with in the meantime? A paid down on a house in town for you.
LEN:	For me?
MAMA:	Yes. A knew that one day you would come home, an' would want a nice place to live.
LEN:	But what money I sent was to fix up this place for yourself.
MAMA:	I soon dead. Where A put the documents? *[She looks for them in the bureau drawer.]* Is a good thing you come. Is over a year now. The house should have been finished, but only last week a letter come asking for more money. Ah, these must be the papers. It is yours so take charge. *[Handing him the documents.]*
LEN:	In the meantime we have to fix up this place, get you a little gas stove.
MAMA:	Gas? Me 'fraid a gas, come blow me up.
LEN:	It is quite safe, Mama, and a little inside bathroom.
MAMA:	So what wrong with mi pit toilet?
LEN:	You deserve to be comfortable, Mama.
MAMA:	I comfortable as it is.
LEN:	More comfortable then, Mama.
MAMA:	I too old to change. Me 'custom to mi pit toilet, an' as a boy you never complain. Is only now that you expose. Nuh fret yuhself 'bout that. Next thing people malice me off, then come lick me down say me live in big house. No, sir! There is more important an' urgent matters we have to discuss. Sit down. *[He does.]* Now about the woman you married. . . . *[LEN is up like a flash.]*
LEN:	Now look here!
MAMA:	Sit down! *[She stands over him commandingly. He sits, as the lights start to fade on the area.]*
PA BEN:	The two a them lock up in the little house for

24

hours. A wonder what they was chatting 'bout,
till mi curiosity got the better a me, and A put mi
ears to the walls. She was right at him 'bout the
woman he married, an' how she obeah him. When
Missa Lenny leave that day, it look like he had one
helluva headache, and the headache travel with
him right back to town, so …

*[He starts the song 'Change the house round'. The other actors join in,
singing the song as a 'round' as they change the set around.]*

Change the house round
To the house in town
So change the house round
To the house in town
Wall to wall carpet on the ground
Big TV set and Frigidaire
Big stuffed sofa and chandelier
Big gramophone with latest sound
But his headache still going round and round.
So change the house etc …

*[MAMA turns the picture on the Down Right wall round, then helps LEN to
turn the old bureau round so that it now serves as LEN's desk. Then she goes
over to PA BEN, sits beside him, all the time singing the song.*

7. ✔

*GEORGE comes on with the telephone and sets it down on the desk/table set
Down Right by LEN and MAMA. Next he sets the coffee table in place, moves
Up Centre, strikes the pelmet and takes it off, then positions himself by the
Up Right door, receiving the chairs from the Stage Manager and passing
them on to PEARL. GEORGE closes the door behind LEN as the change is
completed.*

*PEARL comes on from Up Left, removes the matting that covers MAMA's bench
and takes it off-stage, returning immediately to set the stool beside the bar,
then moves Up Right to collect the chairs from GEORGE, setting them behind
the coffee table.*

*LOIS follows PEARL on with three bottles, three glasses and a box of tablets, sets
up the bar and goes off.*

*LEN helps MAMA to turn the bureau around, then strikes the right panel from
MAMA's house.*

All through this PA BEN sings lustily.

*The Stage Manager strikes the left panel from MAMA's house, receives the
pelmet from GEORGE, hands chairs to GEORGE, and sets book and ice pack*

how to change the set around with the audience watching

[*Stage Right for* LEN's *entrance. The set change happens in a half light. As it is done,* LEN *sits round about Centre Stage.* LOIS *applies an ice pack to his head. The lights come up to full as the singing dies away.*]

LOIS: [*Soothing* LEN's *troubled brow*] How come you're so tense? Relax.

LEN: I am relaxed, except for this headache.

LOIS: Reading won't get rid of it.

LEN: It's the only thing that helps. You know I don't take aspirin.

LOIS: Oh yes, I forgot. What do you take for gripe? *The Reader's Digest*?

LEN: Funny. Ha ha!

LOIS: You think it's funny, eh?

LEN: Very.

LOIS: I guess if I don't laugh, I'll cry. Put the book down and talk to me, Len.

LEN: My head is splitting. [LOIS *tosses the ice pack down on the coffee table.*] I really have a bad headache.

LOIS: Ah well, another weekend with the four walls staring at the back of your head! I wonder what I'll tell the judge? Women lose their husbands for diverse reasons Your Honour: to another woman, occasionally to another man, although that's becoming increasingly more so nowadays, but has a woman ever lost her husband to a book? A book! I name them all as correspondent. [*She goes to him and attempts to caress him sensuously.*] 'Cepting of course anything written on the theme of 'Tender Love', 'Hot Romance', 'Tales of Passion'.

LEN: Lois, please. [*As he pushes her away*] Your endless squawking is creating havoc with the sensitivity of my ear drums.

LOIS: None of you is sensitive, Len.

He's not sexing her.

LEN: Your mind is between you legs.

LOIS: So that's why you don't stimulate me intellectually!

LEN: [*Rising angrily*] One of these days I am going to plug that mouth of yours with a fist or a foot.

LOIS: [*Shouting back at him*] That's what I need you to do. Let some blood … Get this marriage out of its menopause!

LEN: Thank your lucky stars I am not a man given to physical violence.

1.1

LOIS:	You're not given to affection either. I'm off to the beach.
LEN:	Two women got raped there last week.
LOIS:	Something to look forward to.
LEN:	Okay, get my trunks.
LOIS:	*[Comes storming back]* And after the beach, what? Back to bionic bliss with the bionic book man. Back to making whoopee in seventh heaven on a choo choo train that's going no place.
LEN:	You always had a flair for the dramatic, eh?
LOIS:	Why not? Our lives are totally theatrical.
LEN:	Sweetheart …
LOIS:	So that's it for today, folks. Join us again later today for another chapter in this unending life drama. Will Lois Tomlinson find true happiness with the Bionic Black, or will she be forever … *[As she is going off]*
MAMA:	*[From off]* Hold dog!

[LOIS stops, turns, looks at LEN who suddenly becomes very alive, looks in the direction of the 'Hold dog', then towards LOIS. He rushes towards the latter.]

LOIS:	I wish you would impress upon your mother that we do not have a dog.
LEN:	Lois.
LOIS:	Unless of course she is referring to me, which in fact she is.
LEN:	Lois, please.
LOIS:	Excuse me.
LEN:	At least stay and say hello.
LOIS:	Hello.
LEN:	Lois!
MAMA:	*[By the door]* Hold dog! *[LOIS barks like a dog.]*
LEN:	Lois! It's opened, Mama. *[He pleads non-verbally with LOIS as he goes to meet MAMA who has entered.]*
MAMA:	Mass Len.
LEN:	Mama.
MAMA:	Mass Len.
LEN:	Mama.
MAMA:	How you do?
LEN:	Oh fine, Mama. How are you?
MAMA:	Give God thanks.
LEN:	Yes. You looking well.

Christianity

27

1.1

MAMA:	But you don't look too good. A can feel your ribs like something cutting into me. You eating well?
LEN:	Three meals a day.
MAMA:	If you eating three meals as you say, an' yuh face look so haggard, then you must be under stress.
LEN:	Aw, come on, Mama.
MAMA:	Then look on yuh head. Every time A see it, it look like you grey up a little more.
LEN:	The girls like it, say I look distinguished.
MAMA:	*[Hiss]* Nonsense. *[She starts to inspect and clean the furniture.]*
LEN:	Mama *[very discreetly and surreptitiously]*, tell Lois hello.
MAMA:	Ah, Miss Lois.
LOIS:	Miss Simmons. How are you?

[MAMA picks up the ice pack, holds it up disdainfully.]

MAMA:	As well as can be expected under the circumstances.
LOIS:	I see. Now you must excuse me as I have to clean the shit out of the doghouse. *[LOIS smiles. MAMA smiles back. LEN cringes. LOIS goes off.]*
MAMA:	Vulgar wretch! What she smiling with me for, after she not mi friend?
LEN:	Mama, you promised.
MAMA:	I promised to keep the peace. I never promised to be nice to her. It hard to play the hypocrite.
LEN:	Okay, okay.
MAMA:	Tar baby. Every time A come here A come with a heavy heart. When A think of that lovely brown girl with hair down to her back that you could have married. What a distress. *[She shouts off.]* Topsy!
LEN:	Mama!
MAMA:	All right, I will shut mi mouth, but it not easy to bottle it up inside me.
LEN:	Let me get you a drink.
MAMA:	So you is the manservant.
LEN:	What can I get you?
MAMA:	A not thirsty.
LEN:	Actually I am glad you came into town, as I wanted to talk to you rather urgently about the house.
MAMA:	You have some good news for me?

Topsy – a black slave girl (handwritten annotation)

28

LEN:	Not so good, Mama.
MAMA:	Lawd, don't tell me say A going to lose all mi money.
LEN:	There's a chance we could get some, if not all of it back.
MAMA:	Try yuh best, mi son.
LEN:	How did you hear of this housing scheme? Was it advertised in the papers or what?
MAMA:	No. Is Missa Mac encourage me to buy.
LEN:	You mean George McFarlane?
MAMA:	I only know him as Missa Mac.
LEN:	How did this Mister Mac encourage you?
MAMA:	I was in the bank one day, the same bank A had the little savings in. *[LEN faces Up Stage and freezes. MAMA removes her hat, goes into her bag, takes out a red one and puts it on. GEORGE enters.]*
GEORGE:	What a thing, eh?
MAMA:	What?
GEORGE:	The new round of price increases.
MAMA:	Things dear, eh, Missa Mac?
GEORGE:	And they going to get worse.
MAMA:	Don't say so. How poor people going to manage?
GEORGE:	Don't ask me, Miss G. Remember in the good old days? You go to the shop with a shilling and you know what you could buy?
MAMA:	Bread.
GEORGE:	Lard.
MAMA:	Salt beef.
GEORGE:	And you get back change. Now salt beef is three dollars a pound! *[Pointing it out to her as she holds paper.]*
MAMA:	Things can't get no worse.
GEORGE:	Don't fool yourself, Miss G. Next year this time, salt beef could be four dollars a pound.
MAMA:	Hush yuh mouth.
GEORGE:	The hard facts of life. Five years from now, who knows?
MAMA:	These are the last days. *[Returns paper.]* Praise God I won't be here much longer.
GEORGE:	*[Returns to the table and sits on it.]* It may be cheaper to try and stay alive, I tell you. I buried my father-in-law a few weeks back. Cost me the earth,

	thousands of dollars. Old Reverend Greaves must be turning in his grave when he realise the expense he put me to.
MAMA:	Reverend Greaves who used to be the Minister at Sandilands?
GEORGE:	You knew him?
MAMA:	Mi Minister. Good and generous man he was to me and my son. Lord rest his soul. So you got married to Miss Margaret?
GEORGE:	That's right.
MAMA:	Oh, that's all right. I don't feel so bad now.
GEORGE:	Eh?
MAMA:	Just a little something with miself. How is she?
GEORGE:	Very well.
MAMA:	I could see her now. Lovely brown-skin girl with her hair down to her back. She still pretty?
GEORGE:	She is.
MAMA:	She wouldn't remember me now, but tell her howdy for me, from an old friend, and tell her say A sorry to hear about the Reverend. We all did love him.
GEORGE:	He lived with us when he retired. He had to. The little pension he got, with the cost of living as it is today, wasn't enough to buy him food for the week.
MAMA:	Lord, for a man who saved so many souls.
GEORGE:	He was always a thrifty man, mind you. Had put by his few pennies for a rainy day. How was he to know that he would have to cope with this pile of price increases? I warned him; if he had only taken my advice. I was tired of telling him that money in the bank is no use. Let it work for you. Invest. And that is my advice to you too, Miss Simmons. You have too much money in the bank sitting down doing nothing.
MAMA:	But it earning interest.
GEORGE:	Five per cent when the cost of living jumping forty per cent every year?
MAMA:	Advise me.
GEORGE:	Example. If you were to pay down on a little house, three or four years from now you double your money, so when the salt beef go up to five or six

Act 1 Scene 1

	dollars a pound, you right up there with it.
MAMA:	I see yuh point. But the money is for mi son.
GEORGE:	Oh.
MAMA:	Him livin' in England. A get word only last week say he graduate as doctor.
GEORGE:	Nice, nice. You must be proud, eh?
MAMA:	If A proud. One day A know he will come home, and whatever in the bank book belongs to him.
GEORGE:	But think of it, Miss G, and I am not one to put pressure on you, but let's say yuh son come home some time in the future. He goin' to need a nice place to live. Why not use the money to pay down on a place for him? You could rent it out till he come if you don't want to live in it. The rent pays the mortgage. It's a solid investment, no risks.
MAMA:	I know you wouldn't give me bad advice.
GEORGE:	Come to think of it, right at this moment I know of a really good buy going. Nice reasonable price. I know the fellers who are building them. Good honest boys. Go home and think about it. Next week you can let me know if you are interested.
MAMA:	Is God send you here to guide and look after me, you know. Lord, yes, a house for mi son. Lord, yes! Thank you, Missa Mac, thank you. *[Shaking his hand Vigorously. GEORGE goes.]*

[The action returns to the present.]

MAMA:	Missa Mac help me to fill out the papers an' I paid the money. August coming is two years. No money, no house. I been trying to find Missa Mac but him not working at the bank no more.
LEN:	I'll find him.
MAMA:	Yes, he will help you to straighten it out.
LEN:	Leave it to me. But you and this Mr Mac seem to have been quite good friends, how come?
MAMA:	At first I thought it a little odd miself, Mass Len, because is years A been going to the bank and we never had occasion to talk, and anyway I am a lady who know mi place. One day I was in the line and Missa Mac call me out, make the lodgement for me, invite me into his office, offer me refreshment, an' started to talk to me nice, nice. I was surprised, couldn't figure out what this high posh white

31

she is flattered by George's attention to her in the bank; she being Black, he being fair skinned

George took advantage of her because she was Black & she revered fair-skinned people

	gentleman wanted with the likes o' poor little me. Anyway after a few weeks is like we did know each other for years.
LEN:	I think I am beginning to understand, Mama.
MAMA:	Is in your hands, all right?
LEN:	All right.
MAMA:	I have to be going. *[LEN gets up really fast.]* I mustn't overstay mi welcome.
LEN:	You are always welcome here, you know that.
MAMA:	Take care a yuhself. Lawd, every time A look at you water come to mi eye. Look at you. Favour somebody who could be mi husband.
LEN:	*[Hustling her out]* As soon as I have some positive word on the house I'll come and look for you.
MAMA:	Oh Lord, me a leave an' me nuh even give you what A brought for you.
LEN:	Thank you, Mama. *[Taking the parcel which is rather oily.]*
MAMA:	An' I have two nice pigs. One is yours, but I don't suppose you could keep it up here. Mind you, the way Topsy keep the place …
LEN:	Keep him for me.
MAMA:	The pigs friendly, you see! One night A come home from market and A couldn't find them. A look everywhere. Not a sign. I say somebody gone with them. Is when A ready to go to bed, A go to use the chimmy an' see the pigs under the bed fast asleep. *[MAMA laughs. LEN laughs embarrassedly and goes to open the door for her. She, however, is caught up with her memory and continues, unaware that he is no longer beside her.]* A never see pigs friendly so. Them is mi company. *[She becomes aware that he is no longer listening. She covers the slight and goes to the door.]* So you will check with me?
LEN:	Fine.
MAMA:	All right. *[She is going, stops, turns.]* The dog tie?
LEN:	Mama!

Topsy – a black slave girl

insulting Lois

[The lights go down, then come up almost immediately. LOIS in the nice new frock is sitting, reading. A knocking is heard off. LOIS opens the door and calls out.]

LOIS:	Hello.
GEORGE:	Are the dogs tied?

32

Lois:	We don't have a dog. Do come. *[Pause.]*
George:	*[Getting closer]* I saw the sign on the gate.
Lois:	We just haven't bothered to take it down.
George:	*[As he arrives at the door]* Afternoon.
Lois:	Hi.
George:	I am here to see. ... Lois! *[Pause.]*
Lois:	Mr McFarlane?
George:	Surprise, surprise! *[Long pause.]* Aren't you going to invite me in?
Lois:	Come in. This is a bit of a surprise. What are you doing here?
George:	Actually I am here to see a Dr Len Tomlinson. Am I at the right house?
Lois:	Yes. *[Very hesitantly.]*
George:	Are you Mrs ...?
Lois:	Yes.
George:	Really? I had no idea. It's been a long time. Ten years?
Lois:	Thereabouts.
George:	You're looking as well as ever, though. *[Pause.]* So how are things?
Lois:	I mustn't complain.
George:	No. By the look of things, no.
Lois:	And at the bank?
George:	I'm on my own now. Real estate.
Lois:	I see. My husband isn't here. He called saying he would be a few minutes late.
George:	I'll wait. *[Pause.]*
Lois:	I didn't know you two knew each other.
George:	I'm meeting him for the first time.
Lois:	Oh. Can I get you a drink? *[She starts towards the bar.]*
George:	The usual.
Lois:	Mr McFarlane!
George:	No need for us to be formal with each other. George.
Lois:	I ah ... *[Pause.]*
George:	Yes?
Lois:	It's just that ... I'd appreciate if you didn't let on to my husband that we ever knew each other.
George:	*[Pause]* Reasonable.

[The telephone rings. Lois goes across and answers it.]

Lois:	That may be Len again. Hello. ... Yes, he's here.

✓ **10.**

But he does
not wish
him well,
George is
his greatest
malice

	Hold, please.
GEORGE:	Hello … Bertie … say what? What you hear? That is true. I went back *[He notices LOIS]* I can't talk now. *[LOIS sees his distress and goes off.]* Yes, I went back to the bank begging for time. I drew blank. The man say it's out of his hands. Calm down, Bertie. I tell you what, call me at home. No need to panic. … What you think I been doing all day, man, sitting on mi ass? Listen to me, let's not make a decision till I have spoken with this man. Jesus Christ, Bertie, man, calm down. … I know that. The valuator is a buddy of mine. He will hold off on his report for at least two weeks. The man owe me a favour, man. Two weeks is all the time I will need to raise the money. You know doors always open to me, Bertie! I'll get you out. *[GEORGE notices LEN who has come on some time earlier.]* We will talk later. *[He hangs up. The two men stare at each other.]* Dr Tomlinson?
LEN:	Len.
GEORGE:	George McFarlane.
LEN:	I hope I didn't keep you waiting for too long.
GEORGE:	Not at all. Nice place you have here, man.
LEN:	Thank you. You didn't have any trouble finding it?
GEORGE:	I live up the road, number 34.
LEN:	We are neighbours. Imagine that. Nice place you have there too.
GEORGE:	Thank you.
LEN:	I thought we'd meet here. For what I have in mind it makes it more discreet.
GEORGE:	I read you.
LEN:	Drink?
GEORGE:	Scotch.
LEN:	On the rocks?
GEORGE:	Straight.
LEN:	So we finally meet.
GEORGE:	Well, here we are.
LEN:	You are a hard man to find.
GEORGE:	Always on the go.
LEN:	Or under pressure.
GEORGE:	Bit o' both.
LEN:	So I've been hearing. I have my contacts. I bet you

	checked me out too, didn't you?
GEORGE:	You are the new man at the Development Bank.
LEN:	Is that all?
GEORGE:	So far.
LEN:	*[Smiles]* And you are the Managing Director of ABC Homes.
GEORGE:	That is correct.
LEN:	I hear you been having a bit of ill luck.
GEORGE:	It's more than that, man.
LEN:	Explain.
GEORGE:	I think I have an enemy.
LEN:	Don't we all? Ha, ha!
GEORGE:	No, I am convinced somebody is out to get me. I was Bank Manager for Barclays, and a few months ago I was in line for a promotion. I was the best man for the job, but no, I am passed over for some feller with very little experience, so I told Head Office where to get off and resigned. I had a loan or two out with them. You know the spiteful sons of bitches called them in without notice?
LEN:	Other banks would be happy to do business with you, I'm sure.
GEORGE:	Yes, but somebody has put the word out on me. It's like an orchestrated plan to ruin me. Malicious, insidious lies are being spread around.
LEN:	I've heard one or two.
GEORGE:	Don't believe a word they tell you. What you heard?
LEN:	If they are lies as you say, why repeat them?
GEORGE:	True, true. *[He laughs foolishly.]* Something you might have heard that could have some truth to it is that I do need a bit of refinancing.
LEN:	I represent a group of investors. They suggested that I talk to you.
GEORGE:	Who are these boys?
LEN:	They want to keep a low profile for the time being. In the event that you and I get to first base, then they'd want to get into the picture.
GEORGE:	I see.

[LEN takes GEORGE's glass to get a refill.]

LEN:	What would you give as the rough estimates of the assets of ABC at this time?

rumours (may have been spread by Len)

GEORGE:	About three million.
LEN:	Dollars?
GEORGE:	Give or take a thou or two.
LEN:	Let's get a valuation. *[GEORGE dips into his briefcase and comes out with some papers. He hands them to LEN.]* I see you came prepared.
GEORGE:	For any eventualities.
LEN:	Estimated profit, twenty-five per cent. Who worked out these figures?
GEORGE:	My appraisers.
LEN:	I'll get one of my appraisers to do a valuation. *[GEORGE daps into his briefcase again and hands another set of papers to LEN.]* You've been anticipating me. Estimated profit down to ten per cent on this one.
GEORGE:	Your valuators always undervalue.
LEN:	One or two other things.
GEORGE:	A recognised auditor to go over the cash flow. *[He dips into his briefcase again for another set of papers.]*
LEN:	Profit margins down to only five per cent now. Looking at these figures I'd say, of hand, that my group wouldn't be willing to offer you more than eight hundred thousand dollars at the most; if you had to sell, that is.
GEORGE:	What? At that price I would come out with less than nothing.
LEN:	I appreciate your position. If you don't get refinanced, chances are the bank will put this place up for auction, and where would that leave you?
GEORGE:	Shit! Eight hundred thousand … *[Pause.]* Maybe we could work something out between us, personal.
LEN:	What you have in mind?
GEORGE:	How about a piece o' my action?
LEN:	How big a piece, and what do I have to do for it?
GEORGE:	Finance me through your bank for thirty per cent of the profits.
LEN:	Hmm. Tempting.
GEORGE:	With financing, ABC could be a gravy train, a money machine. For example, here is a list of prospective purchasers willing to purchase at an escalated price.
LEN:	And the people who bought already?

GEORGE:	They pay the escalated price, or get their money back.
LEN:	Let me think about it.
GEORGE:	I don't have much time.
LEN:	I know that. I am going to need some more information on ABC, how it is structured, that sort of thing.
GEORGE:	First thing in the morning.
LEN:	Beautiful. Another Scotch?
GEORGE:	Yes, sir. *[Breathing easier.]*
LEN:	George, you know I am sure I know you from some place.
GEORGE:	I don't think so.
LEN:	From where? Let me think. Canada?
GEORGE:	No. Never been to Canada.
LEN:	I never forget a face. Munro old boy?
GEORGE:	Yeah.
LEN:	'41?
GEORGE:	That's right. You went to Munro?
LEN:	You left in '47?
GEORGE:	Yeah.
LEN:	That's it! I know you man. Remember me, Len Tomlinson?
GEORGE:	Len Tomlinson? Oh yeah. *[He most decidedly has not remembered LEN.]*
LEN:	Vague, vague. I was in a lower form. Man, you haven't changed a day. *[Snaps his finger.]* Mongoose!
GEORGE:	Jesus! *[laughs]* Look, nuh, man, not a soul's called me Mongoose in years! *[laughs]]* Jesus Christ!
LEN:	Remember me now?
GEORGE:	Yes man. *[He still hasn't.]*
LEN:	No matter, no matter. It'll all come back; it's been thirty years. We must talk and talk, roll back the years. To the old school, and those of us who have survived. 'Benedictus benedicat, per Jesum Christum dominum nostrum.' *[They drink.]*
GEORGE:	Some say chicken, some say duck, we say matron don't wut a fa, fa, fa, fa …
LEN:	Same old Mongoose! How is the old school? I haven't been back in years.
GEORGE:	Place is completely changed. Packed now with a bunch o' riffraff' scholarship-winners. Sacred walls,

[handwritten margin notes: telling the actor to show how he does not remember him; profanity; 'May the blessed one bless (the food and us), through Jesus Christ, our Lord.']

man, desecrated. I was there on Sports Day. My boy won the hundreds.

LEN: Chip off the old block, eh?

GEORGE: You remember?

LEN: How could I forget?

GEORGE: Class One champ. On your marks, get set … Those were the days! God damn it to hell, the good old days! They'll never come back. *[A noise is heard outside.]* What's that?

[LEN listens; GEORGE draws his gun.]

LEN: I think it's the wife tinkering outside.

GEORGE: Oh boy. I am a nervous wreck. *[Putting his gun back.]* Life has very little pleasure for me today, what with all the fear, the violence, the social upheaval, the economic mismanagement. My house is like a prison, so many bolts on the door. If I lost the key I would have to sell the place! The family alone at home. Jesus! I can use yuh phone?

LEN: Sure. *[Pointing to the instrument.]*

GEORGE: *[On telephone]* Billy? Daddy. Where's your mother? … Don't worry to wake her. You locked up the house? Lock all the windows. *[Shouting]* I say you must lock all the windows! I soon come. *[He hangs up.]* Can't be too careful these days. They broke into next door 7.30 one evening, lucky nobody was there, ransack the place, rape the maid. You see this, *[taking out the gun]* I declare war! I tell my wife, 'You get diarrhoea at night, wake me up, wake me up!'. For I am going to shoot first and ask questions afterwards. You have one of these? *[Indicating the gun.]*

LEN: No.

GEORGE: *[Getting more and more like a scared trapped animal]* What, man? Get one! An' put some bars on those windows! This place is like a death trap! Not even a dog?

LEN: We should. We should.

GEORGE: Violence. Socialism. Shit! If I wasn't a damn ass I would have been living in Toronto years ago! I tell you, I would rather be a second-class citizen in the first world, than a first-class one in this rat's ass place. I can help myself? *[As he goes to the bottle.]*

To him, the maid is nobody

LEN:	Sure. Stay for supper.
GEORGE:	Thanks, but not this evening. The wife would have left supper. Come to think of it, you should know Margaret.
LEN:	Margaret? Margaret?
GEORGE:	Greaves. Reverend Greaves daughter from school days.
LEN:	You and Margaret, married?
GEORGE:	Yes, man.
LEN:	What a thing!
GEORGE:	We been going together from school days.
LEN:	I had no idea that you two … Mmm … Really! Hey, you remember Blackie?
GEORGE:	Blackie? I wonder if it's the same boy I am thinking of, can't remember his name. Bright little boy. Won scholarship.
LEN:	Could be.
GEORGE:	Must have been as poor as ass, though. Clothes patch, socks have hole. We boys use to give him hell. *[Laughs]* Those days. Blackie. One Open Day … It wasn't Blackie we called him, though? Anyway, it was Open Day, the other parents came in car an' buggy an' thing, an' when we look through the window, we saw this boy's mother coming up the hill with a basket on her head. The thing full of bananas, yams, cocos, all sort of things for the lad. The boy had a gut, you see, man, could eat! Man, I am telling you, as she was coming through the door, she miss her step an' everything in that basket was rolling all over the place! The headmaster didn't know what to do! At the time I think he was chatting to the Chairman of the Board, and one of the totos rolled right between his legs. When he look down and saw the toto sitting lopsided-like down there; man, the Chairman was just about to look down when the Head's foot ease across and cover the toto. All this time the poor boy an' his mother was busy going around collecting all the foodstuff, the other boys and parents noticing them, but not noticing them, you know what I mean. What a laugh! Weeks afterwards. *[He laughs.]* You remember it?

prejudice

LEN:	I remember it. *[Laughing.]*
GEORGE:	The boy didn't know what to do with himself. From that day, they call him 'Toto'. But wait a minute, that's not Blackie. Might have been the same boy. Was funny, you see?
LEN:	You really don't remember me at all, do you, George?
GEORGE:	Yes, man.
LEN:	Toto. Toto Tomlinson. Who else? Me.
GEORGE:	Oh shit!
LEN:	That's all right.
GEORGE:	I didn't realise.
LEN:	How could you? It's been years.
GEORGE:	How is your mother now?
LEN:	Not too good, George, seeing as how you owe her three thousand dollars on the house deal.
GEORGE:	Boy, I hadn't realised.
LEN:	Forget it, man, a little joke at my expense. What's a little joke between old friends? Who laughed loudest? Me. Man, it's so damn nice to see you. Ah Lois, come and join us. You met George?
LOIS:	Yes, I did.
GEORGE:	Hello again.
LEN:	Another drink?
GEORGE:	Thanks, but actually I have to run. *[Gathering up his papers, briefcase, etc.]*
LEN:	First thing in the morning?
GEORGE:	Ah, yes.
LEN:	Take care. 'Night.
GEORGE:	'Night.
LOIS:	'Bye.

[As GEORGE goes, LEN closes the door and he laughs and laughs.]

LOIS:	Len! *[LEN cannot contain himself laughing.]*
LEN:	Let's go upstairs and I'll tell you all about it. *[As they are going, LEN stops and turns to the door that GEORGE went out through.]* Son of a bitch!

END OF ACT ONE

Hatred
uncertainty

40

Act Two

Scene One

11 ✓

[In the darkness we hear the voices of the actors/villagers questioning who has brought the peanuts, teasing each other, a general hubbub, noisy and carefree. A match explodes in the darkness as PA BEN lights his pipe.]

PA BEN:	All right, all right. *[Checking and showing his bottle of rum.]* A ready for you again. Settle off, settle off, while A get mi head together. Where A did reach?
ACTRESS WHO PLAYS MAMA:	Where Missa Lenny was laughing.
PA BEN:	Ah yes. What a way it did sweet him! Him laugh till him almost wet him pants, but you hear what they say, 'What sweet nanny goat. ...' *[All the actors/villagers join in – 'A go run him belly'.]* Miss Lois anxious to know what sweet him so and what happen between him and the one McFarlane.
ACTOR WHO PLAYS GEORGE:	What secret Mongoose carrying for Miss Lois?
PA BEN:	Miself want to know.
ALL THE ACTORS/ VILLAGERS:	You know, man, you know.
ACTOR WHO PLAYS LEN:	Yes, him know.
PA BEN:	I don't know, honest, would I tell a lie?
ALL THE ACTORS/ VILLAGERS:	Yes.
PA BEN:	What I do know is that if Missa Lenny did know, maybe him wouldn't laugh so. Anyway that same night Missa Lenny tell Miss Lois everything about the one Mongoose.
ACTRESS WHO PLAYS PEARL:	Everything?
PA BEN:	Well not quite everything. Him leave out a very important piece o' the story.
ACTOR WHO PLAYS LEN:	What him leave out?
PA BEN:	Not just what, but why.
ALL THE ACTORS/ VILLAGERS:	So tell us. Tell us. *[They keep demanding.]*
PA BEN:	*[He gets up from his storytelling area and walks a little right.]* Patience, everything in its time. Him tell her

suspense

As the storyteller, he has the ability to withhold information until he's ready to release it.

41

some of what happen in schooldays. How the boy
McFarlane did dunce. Missa Lenny remember it as
if it was yesterday. No, Missa Lenny never forget
Mongoose and all the other big shot boys them.

*[During the above speech the actor playing GEORGE dresses himself in a black
and red cape, black on the outside, and dons a flamboyant red cap. Armed
with his riding crop he mounts the storyteller's chair and sits on the back, his
feet resting on the seat. Two of the actors turn slowly towards the audience
becoming the horses to GEORGE's buggy. The actor playing LEN dresses himself
in a much less flamboyant red cap, then waits Up Right of the storyteller's
area. The transition happens smoothly and there is no break in the action.]*

On the one or two occasion that I had occasion to
accompany Miss Aggy up to the school, me miself
remember seeing the Hi Poshers riding into the
school yard in them shiny new buggies with the
big black stallions in harness – kippity kop, kippity
kop.

*[The actor playing LEN makes the sound of the 'kippity kop' using two
coconut shells. The actress playing MAMA jangles a chain for the effect of the
bridle, etc. All the odd bits of clothes and the effects are brought on in the
darkness at the beginning of Act Two.]*

GEORGE: *[On buggy riding away]* Giddy yap!
PA BEN: You should see them, just sneering down on the
world, them head way up in the sky, drunk with
power and authority.
GEORGE: Whoa. *[He dismounts.]*
PA BEN: But is when they start to strut roun' like peacock,
the fat slobs them dress up in they Sunday go-to-
meeting. Biggitty, oh so arrogant!

[GEORGE struts around still dressed in his finery.]

GEORGE: Here, boy. *[LEN hesitates.]* On the double, boy!
Move! *[LEN hurries.]* Clean my shoes, burnish it till
you see your big black ugly face in it, boy! *[LEN goes
on all fours and starts to polish GEORGE's shoe. GEORGE
is enjoying himself immensely. He uses LEN's back as a
foot-rest for his free foot, his riding crop poised over LEN's
backside.]* And boy, don't forget we need you for
the Easter play. We have you down for three parts
– Judas Iscariot, one of the thieves, and both ends
of the donkey. Ha, ha, ha! *[He straddles LEN, riding
and whipping him.]* Sport, what sport!

42

Act 2 Scene 1

[The action freezes after a little while.]

PA BEN: Yeah, you hear what they use him for? They beat
him black behind till it turn blue, all o' them
playing Jesus, and they ride him into Jerusalem!
I don't forget them, and Missa Lenny don't forget
them either. It live in him memory. *[PA BEN calls
the actress who played PEARL. He whispers to her and she
goes off, excitedly.]* Dere it was, Miss Aggy spend her
good money to educate the boy, and he pass good
good, but him couldn't get no job in the bank,
only manual labour.

*[During the above speech, GEORGE dismounts and very haughtily takes
off his cape and cap. He hands them to LEN, along with his riding crop.
GEORGE walks into the bank area, which is to the right. On the chair behind
the table, his coat and tie have been set during the interval. Back to the
audience, he puts them on. LEN goes off with cape, crop and cap, returning
to put the chairs back in place behind the coffee table. PA BEN's line Only
manual labour coincides with this action. The action is continuous, no
break.]*

But duncey Mongoose who never pass one subject
never had to ask for no job. No, they ask him if
him want the job. Him who didn't even know
enough to work in Missa Elias cloth shop, and
they give him the keys to the vault. In no time at
all, him move from Teller to Bank Manager. In a
few years him end up rich rich. I couldn't figure
it out so I had to ask Missa Lenny to explain it to
me, and the way I understand it … Suppose you
want to start a housing scheme, you going to need
money to borrow, so you go to George's bank.

[GEORGE dials a number and is talking quietly on the telephone.]

GEORGE: Yes, Bertie, up to now the wife is none the wiser.
*[He laughs. as the actress who played PEARL enters
GEORGE's office as the REAL ESTATE DEVELOPER.]* Hang On,
Bertie. *[To DEVELOPER]* Are you the lady from the
Real Estate Development Company?

DEVELOPER: I am.

GEORGE: Let's see the plans. *[She displays them on the coffee
table, inadvertently laying the plans upside down. GEORGE
looks them over.]* Ah ha … hmm. Yes.

PA BEN: Him only looking. Him don't understand nutten.

	[The DEVELOPER seeing the plans upside down turns them round.]
GEORGE:	Oh. *[Laughs foolishly.]* Hmm. Hmm. I see. Not bad, not bad. I'll have to put this up to head office, see what they think. Leave everything and check back with me next week. *[Hustling her out. GEORGE resumes his telephone conversation. He is very excited.]* Bertie boy, I am on to something hot, a housing scheme development! It's brilliant! Contact the other boys, we have to meet later. Financing will be no problem. Contact our lawyer friend, same contract as last time.
PA BEN:	Sly. No wonder they call him Mongoose.
GEORGE:	Man, we could make a million off this one. I don't know how I didn't think of it before. I was sitting here and the thing just flash in front of my eyes.
PA BEN:	Liar.
GEORGE:	Now, about a name for this new company, Bertie. We going to need something really profound, like ahm let me see. How about A.B.C. Homes?
PA BEN:	Damn! I could call it that. A.B.C.
GEORGE:	Homes. That's it man, you like it? Good, good. You see the symbolism?
PA BEN:	So when next week come and the woman go back to see what happening with her plan …
GEORGE:	*[On phone]* Tell her I am out.
PA BEN:	Damn lie.
GEORGE:	And head office turned down her proposal.
PA BEN:	Wicked brute.
GEORGE:	But if she come up with anything else, she must check with me.
ACTRESS WHO PLAYS LOIS:	Him want to t'ief her again.
PA BEN:	Now him have the plan, him need to get money to develop it. Him can't borrow it in him own name for him is the bank manager, so him go roun' the corner an' set up him friends to borrow it in their name; one of the friend name Bertie. At the same time George draw up papers with them giving himself seventy per cent of the profit, and the profits keep rolling in.
GEORGE:	*[On phone, sits on the sofa, one foot up on the coffee*

	table, a huge cigar in his hand.] Bertie, contact the lawyers. We need to set up two more companies, same plan as before. *[He hangs up, then pulls on his cigar, savouring it.]*
PA BEN:	Greed married to ignorance. Him try it once too often. The bank find him out. *[GEORGE looks around furtively, puts out his cigar, foot off the coffee table.]* The newspapers hear about it, an' before you know it, Mongoose name gone abroad, *[The actors/villagers sing 'Sly Mongoose, yuh name gone abroad …* oooh!'*]* and is panic in a him pants.

[GEORGE is up and about like a scared mongoose in a cage.]

GEORGE:	Jesus Christ, Bertie, man! All right, all right, don't panic. Advertise them again. We have to sell twelve houses this week or we are in plenty trouble! Yes, I read the article. Somebody should burn down that newspaper. Who the hell could have fed them that information? No matter, if we organise we can come out. Leave it to me, I have an idea. *[As he looks across to the files in the bookcase.]*
PA BEN:	And that is when George start to forage into people's bank accounts.
ACTRESS WHO PLAYS MAMA:	Forage? You mean t'ief.
PA BEN:	Me mean t'ief. Poor Miss Aggy was only one of the people that him trick.
ACTOR WHO PLAYS LEN:	Ol' tree card man.
PA BEN:	Before you know it, the bank kick him out. Of course they wasn't going to shame one a dem own in public but dem demand back di money him did borrow, and in two twos him start to lose him shirt. *[The actors/villagers sing 'Sly mongoose, yuh name gone abroad … oooh', as they go off.]*
PA BEN:	*[To the audience]* Missa Lenny investigate Mongoose down to the last. Him is a smart boy now, that Missa Lenny. Him got the mongoose in a cage, but A don't like it. When you got a mongoose lock up, is then him dangerous. And that thing with Miss Lois, A don't like it at all. *[He goes into his house.]*

[GEORGE appears on the lower level down right. He is on the telephone, dressed as he was at the end of Act One.]

(handwritten margin notes: "profanity" and "(Len)")

prejudice,
feels he
has power
since he
is fair
skinned

b. ✓

GEORGE:	Yes, Bertie, man, the man Tomlinson is a definite possibility. Is a black man, I can handle him. Plus, and this is a real plus, I know his wife. Ha, ha! We will talk. Look up the files on ABC, a Mrs Tomlinson, tell me where she live. *[Pause]*

[LEN and LOIS come on in their area.]

LEN:	I've been chasing the bugger for months. Ignores my calls; stroke of genius how I got him to come here tonight.
LOIS:	How did you?
LEN:	I put the word out that the new man, Tomlinson, at the bank was a soft touch for a loan, that I wasn't unapproachable about making a deal – under the table, of course. He arrives here tonight with one set of hocus-pocus information. Where is that list of people who he says would be willing to purchase at an escalated price? *[He goes off to get it.]*
GEORGE:	*[On phone]* Say what, no Mrs Tomlinson on the file? There must be, unless … All right, I know how I can get the information. Any luck with tomorrow's pay bill? Oh no! You try your uncle? Anybody we can borrow from? If everything else fails there is a lawyer who can give me a second mortgage on my mother's house. Get a message to the office. Tell the workmen the paybill will be a few hours late an' tell the office staff half pay till Wednesday. I know we won't have it on Wednesday, but then we can think of something else. You have Tomlinson's phone number on you? Let me have it.
LEN:	*[Coming on with the papers]* Here we are, Peter Malcolm; this man died five years ago. I'd say Mr Malcolm's got all the real estate he is likely to need. All fictitious characters.
LOIS:	If he's down and out as you say he is, aren't you wasting your time trying to get your mother's money back?
LEN:	Maybe, but McFarlane is vermin. I have a moral right to rid society of that sort of scum. Come to think of it, you should know McFarlane.
LOIS:	Should I?
GEORGE:	*[On the phone]* Six, eight … *[He records the number as he gets it from Bertie.]*

To render
evil for
evil

46

LEN:	You didn't run into him when you worked at Barclays?
LOIS:	What branch was he at?
LEN:	Uptown.
LOIS:	I was downtown.
GEORGE:	[On phone] Tomorrow.
LEN:	Were you?
LOIS:	Does it matter?
LEN:	Not really. Thought you may have known the bum.

[The phone rings in LEN's house. LOIS answers.]

LOIS:	Hello.
GEORGE:	Lois?
LOIS:	Yes.
GEORGE:	Len's mother, is she a Tomlinson as well? Tell me where she live.
LOIS:	Wrong number. *[She hangs up. The lights go down very slowly on all the areas. In the darkness, LOIS and LEN leave the stage. GEORGE removes his jacket. As the lights come up again he is walking towards PA BEN's house.]*
GEORGE:	*[Calling out]* Hello, hello, anybody at home?
PA BEN:	*[From inside his house]* Is who dat now?
GEORGE:	Come here, man.
PA BEN:	*[Coming out to see GEORGE]* All well. All well. *[He has on his spectacles and there is an open bible in his hand.]*
GEORGE:	Miss Agatha Simmons, where I find her?
PA BEN:	Simmons, Simmons?
GEORGE:	Yeah, Simmons.
PA BEN:	Oh, Miss Aggy. You in the right place, but she not here right now. She just gone down by the Baptist Church. If you walk fast you will catch her, straight ahead. *[GEORGE goes.]* Hey man, you forget something.
GEORGE:	What?
PA BEN:	To tell me thanks.
GEORGE:	Oh, sorry, man. Thanks. *[He goes off left on the lower level.]*
PA BEN:	Rude, no manners, an' 'manners maketh man'. *[To audience]* No, mi spirit never take to him. Never like the looks of the fellow. A wonder what him want with Miss Aggy. She so cagey nowadays, nuh tell me her business like first time. It strange all the same to see a big white man in these parts an' is

nuh election time. A just hope is nuh something bad. *[He looks in the direction* Geᴏʀɢᴇ *left in, then goes into his house.]*

Act Two

Scene Two

14

[As Pa Ben goes in the lights come up on Len in his living area. His jacket is thrown over a chair, his shoes are off. Very relaxedly he is going over George's dossier.]

LEN:	Damn crook!

[Mama is heard knocking off.]

MAMA:	Hold dog!
LEN:	Oh no! Not her with that nonsense again. *[He puts the dossier down and is going towards the door, when he stops, returns fast, puts on shoes, scrambles into his jacket. Mama knocks again.]* Coming, Mama. *[He packs his briefcase quickly and leaves with it to the door. Opening the door]* I wish you wouldn't do that, Mama.
MAMA:	Do what?
LEN:	That 'Hold dog' nonsense.
MAMA:	But you have a sign outside.
LEN:	Okay, Mama. *[He checks his watch.]*
MAMA:	You going out? *[She walks in and sits on Stage Right chair.]*
LEN:	Yes, I have this important meeting.
MAMA:	Don't tell me now say you so busy, you don't even have time to tell me howdy and greet me properly?
LEN:	*[Pecks her on cheek.]* How are you, Mama?
MAMA:	Thank God for life; I should've been up since yesterday, but I had to go to a funeral. You 'member Miss Pearl?
LEN:	Pearl?
MAMA:	Miss Esmeralda daughter. She dead yesterday, dead in childbirth. The baby live, though. *[Len looks at his watch and Mama notices.]* Anyway, I see you in a hurry, so I won't keep you. *[With great pleasure]* So you couldn't come an' tell me that you saw Missa Mac?
LEN:	*[Very surprised]* Who told you that?
MAMA:	Missa Mac himself come down to see me yesterday.
LEN:	Oh? *[He puts down the briefcase and sits on edge of table.]*
MAMA:	Yes, sit down off in mi kitchen. Big big Missa Mac,

49

comfortable as anything. Him tell me say he saw you, and how him explain everything to you 'bout the house. How him not working at the bank no more.

LEN: Yes?

MAMA: And say that the people he did recommend to me to buy the house from was one bunch a crooks, let him down bad bad, and since he couldn't sit back and see me lose my whole life's savings, he buy them out, and he managing it now. You should see him telling it to me. [*LEN laughs.*] What you laughing at so?

LEN: It's all right; go on, Mama.

MAMA: Only say that right now him in a little financial difficulty, but give him a little time and everything will be all right, but I explain to him that he don't have to worry 'bout my couple pennies, just straighten out his own business first. Since I know is Missa Mac in charge, I know my money safe.

LEN: Mama. [*She gets up and walks to him.*]

MAMA: You know what is a comfort and a blessing to me now, Len?

LEN: What is, Mama?

MAMA: That it turn 'round that now you can help Missa Mac.

LEN: He said that?

MAMA: Yes, he say how you contact him, offer him help.

LEN: Let me explain that to you, Mama.

MAMA: Is a good opportunity to repay the debt we owe the family. His father-in-law feed you when I was down and out. I remember and I am grateful.

LEN: You heard the rumours about him, Mama?

rumours

MAMA: And don't you repeat them. You have more sense than that. Missa Mac warn me, how people out in the street plotting against him. Scandal and malicious lies.

LEN: No, Mama.

MAMA: Shut yuh ears to wickedness, you hear me?

LEN: Listen to me for a while.

Len has no reason to help Mrs. Margaret now; she is married; Len is.

MAMA: No! Black people too wicked and bad. Missa Mac say you could help him. If not for him, then for Miss Margaret. Is God send you this opportunity.

Len is angry when Mama tells him that he owes the Greaves' family for what they did for him (which was not much). He has resentful memories of them which is blinding him from the things that matter most to him (Lois, Mama).

Act 2 Scene 2 (2.2)

	Help them for Mama's sake.
LEN:	*[Taking papers out of his briefcase]* Read some of this.
MAMA:	Some of what? *[She looks at it, then pushes it away.]* Move it from me. Is Miss Margaret father help make you what you is today!

she is inordinately grateful

LEN:	You damn right about that! *[He throws the dossier on the coffee table.]*
MAMA:	Where is yuh gratitude?
LEN:	Gratitude for what? For the two scraps from their table?
MAMA:	Jesus, Saviour, hold mi hand!

Christianity

LEN:	When they eat and leave they throw it to me in the kitchen, like I was a damn stray.

They look down on him

MAMA:	You did want to eat with them 'round the table? You did give dem anyt'ing to put down? They didn't have to give you anything, you know. You should know yuh place. You was always too uppitty.
LEN:	Jesus Christ! Is time you stop bow down an' worship them people like them was God.

profanity

Christianity

MAMA:	Take this cross, Saviour!
LEN:	Them nuh God!
MAMA:	*[Sitting]* Oh Lord, forgive him!

Christianity

LEN:	Set them up on pedestal. I tired of it.
MAMA:	Shut yuh mouth!
LEN:	I've had enough!
MAMA:	*[Shouting at him]* Shut it, I say! If it wasn't for Miss Margaret Pa, you wouldn't get to go to Englan' to come back here to spit on my head, and refuse them help.

Bible reference = Lazarus

LEN:	Help? If it was a damn drop o' water I had to give them to save they life, they woulda dead. You hear me, dead!
MAMA:	You think you too big for me to drop hand on you? *[She grabs him by his jacket and pulls him to her. He breaks her hold, then picks up a chair to hit her, but he stays his hand.]* Ooh. Jesus. Lawd, you see what you come to do? Kill me. Kill me. *[She spins him round.]* You mad? You see what you threaten to do? You realise now say something wrong with you. Woi! The boy pick up chair to kill him ma!

He is so resentful, he attempts to hurt her

LEN:	I'm sorry, Mama. *[As he sits rather disconsolately.]*

[Handwritten annotation, left margin:] She is not forgiving in contrast to her Christian-like nature. She cannot forgive Len like Lois will forgive her.

MAMA: Sorry? Sorry can't help situation. You always sorry. Like for the years you did barely write to me, tie me out in the wilderness and all you could say is you sorry. Same thing when you married, and is one year after you send come tell me. Why you married her? Is like you married her and you can't say why. Is like one morning you wake up, and plops, you married.

LEN: Jesus Christ, Mama, you coming with that again? *[Handwritten: profanity]*

[Handwritten annotation, left margin:] Pa Ben kept his friendship with mama going thus eventually causing her to acknowledge being wrong

MAMA: I must come up with it again, Len *[As she strides over to him.]* What else you expect me to say? I can't forget the day news come say you married. Black Sambo pose off with you in wedding picture. Lawd, against my better judgement I keep the peace, but after your performance here today, raise yuh hand to kill yuh Ma, there is no power on God's earth could convince me say is not obeah *[Handwritten: obeah]* that woman obeah you. *[During the above it is as if MAMA is a woman possessed with great religious fervour. By the end of the scene, the spirits that move her are in total control of mind and body.]*

LEN: Mama! *[He gets up to hold and implore her.]*

[Handwritten annotation, left margin:] Christianity John 8:32

MAMA: *[As she holds him with great urgency]* Len, Len, son, listen to me, son. Your soul is in bondage! A have to release you! A have to set you free!

[LEN stands transfixed. The lights go down on them.]

[Handwritten annotation, left margin:] She does not know the truth (George), is mistaken & jeopardising herself

[Handwritten annotation:] John 8:32 - and you will know the truth & the truth will set you free

Act Two

2.3

Scene Three

15

[Ten seconds or so later. LEN is with PA BEN at PA BEN's house. LEN is in a great state of agitation. He sits, he stands, he walks, turns, etc.]

LEN: And so I came right away, sir.

PA BEN: Settle your nerves. Drink one, drink one. *[Gives LEN the bottle. LEN drinks. The over hundred per cent proof rum throws him into a tizzy.)*

LEN: Ooh!

PA BEN: See what I mean. It take your mind off things.

LEN: *[With hardly any voice.]* Any water, sir?

PA BEN: Don't use it, 'cept to cook with and clean miself. Where Miss Aggy now?

LEN: I left her in town.

PA BEN: Praises be, the sun gone down. She can't do anything till tomorrow.

LEN: Isn't there a man one could go to for protection?

PA BEN: There's one right here in the district.

LEN: That's too close to home. You don't know any a bit further away?

Len doesn't want to risk the spreading of rumours by visiting the man

PA BEN: What you want him for?

LEN: Could you go to him for me?

PA BEN: What for?

LEN: To get some protection for Lois.

PA BEN: Is that you come down here to ask me? I thought you come to ask my advice. Is not protection you want. You want to get your mama to stay her hand.

LEN: That's not possible, sir. If you knew anyone you could go to, I'd really appreciate …

PA BEN: Even if I did know anybody, Miss Lois would have to go for herself. But that's not the answer. You got to soften up your mother and give Mongoose the money.

Pa Ben is trying to kill the malice Len is showing towards George & Mama

LEN: No sir. No, no, no, no. *[Pause.]* No!

PA BEN: I heard the first 'no'. I not deaf. Tell me something, you know what will happen if your mama carry out her threat?

LEN: That's why I have to protect Lois, sir.

PA BEN: And what happens to your mother? You goin' to leave her wide open for the boomerang?

LEN: Boomerang? What's that? I never heard about that.

obeah

PA BEN:	You're a scientist, but you don't study high science yet. Depending on what your mother set off on Miss Lois, whether she just out to get her out of your life or …
LEN:	Or what, sir?
PA BEN:	I can't bring miself to say it, boy. This is no joke. You never can tell how the chips goin' fly. Obeah is a serious thing. Don't meddle with it. You have to stop yuh mother!
LEN:	How?
PA BEN:	I just tell you. *[LEN hesitates. PA BEN pauses.]* Is two ladies in yuh life. You love them? Answer me.
LEN:	Yes, sir.
PA BEN:	Well, then, you can't expose none o' them to this kind of danger. If you don't stop her you have a good chance of losing one o' dem. Now tell me, what more important to you – mashin' up Mongoose life, or would you rather sacrifice one of the women you love? What it is between you and him, anyway?
LEN:	What I told you.
PA BEN:	No. Piece o' the story missin'. If not, your heart couldn't set so against him. If you pay up before she go to the obeah man it could work out.
LEN:	Could!
PA BEN:	Is the chance you have to take. Take the pressure off Miss Lois. If yuh mind is that set against the white feller, then you got to think of something else, an' quick.
LEN:	You think you could talk to her again?
PA BEN:	And say what? The mood you say she in it would be a waste of time. *[Pause.]* Like mother, like son. Two a you stubborn like ol' mule. Supposing …
LEN:	What sir?
PA BEN:	No. *[Pause.]* What a dilemma you come lay on my doorstep this day of our Lord! You don't have any idea?
LEN:	I'm thinking.
PA BEN:	Think fast. *[Pause.]* The other day when me and you had the little argument and you was telling me 'bout the work you do.
LEN:	Yes sir.

Pa Ben is trying to make Len see what is more important to him

PA BEN:	You did explain to me 'bout a thing name computer, solve all kind o' problem. It couldn't help you with this?
LEN:	I'm afraid not, sir.
PA BEN:	So you see, you have science and science. *[Pause.]* Miss Lois suspect any of what going on?
LEN:	Not about this. Look, whatever we do has to be without her knowledge.
PA BEN:	If you don't tell her and you don't stop your mother, confusion.
LEN:	There's always the chance Mama might not …
PA BEN:	Don't fool yourself, join hands with Miss Lois. She may have the solution to the problem.
LEN:	What could I say to her?
PA BEN:	The truth.
LEN:	Lois, my mother is … ahm … planning to put a hex on you. That's what you want me to say?
PA BEN:	Hex? What name hex? It name obeah.
LEN:	This is 1980, sir. The whole thing is ridiculous.
PA BEN:	What the year have to do with it? Is your roots and they grow deep! Don't be ashamed of them! Miss Lois is roots too. She'll understand. Depending on how much love, trust and understanding there is between you, the greater the chance you have of fighting this thing. You have to stop yuh Ma, boy.
LEN:	Till I can think of some way to do that, I have to protect Lois. She is the innocent in all this.
PA BEN:	So is your mother.
LEN:	No, sir, that's ignorance.
PA BEN:	Born and bred of what?
LEN:	At this point I just don't care.
PA BEN:	Well, I care and you better care too.
LEN:	Right now I have to find a way that Lois doesn't go stark raving mad or worse. If you know somebody, give me the name.
PA BEN:	You make yuh choice then?
LEN:	You know the hell I've been through with Mama.
PA BEN:	So be it. I finish. I wash my hands.
LEN:	Mama took her chance, she knew the consequences. *[Pause.]* Didn't she? *[Pause.]* Give me a break, sir.
PA BEN:	There's a lady in town on Mountain View Road by the almond tree, with a flag in her yard. She name

[handwritten margin note: 1980]

[handwritten margin note: Len is not caring about his mother & saying she got what she deserves]

Pa Ben didn't want to have to tell him about Mother Rachael

	Mother Rachael. *[He goes into his house.]*
LEN:	Thank you, sir. *[LEN is going but stops, then returns to knock on PA BEN's windows. PA BEN opens it.]*
PA BEN:	Yes?
LEN:	One last favour. Go see her for me, sir?
PA BEN:	That you have to do for yourself, boy. *[As he tries to close the window.]*
LEN:	*[Hanging on to the window.]* Sir, consider my position at the bank, my reputation. People see a man like me going into a place like that! You want to see me ruined, sir?
PA BEN:	You is the one who need protection, from yourself!

[PA BEN slams the windows shut.]

LEN:	Oh no! *[He goes. In a little while, PA BEN comes out again and looks at LEN disappearing. He shakes his head sucking in on his teeth, when he hears MAMA coming from the opposite direction on the lower level.]*
PA BEN:	All well. All well.
MAMA:	*[Sullenly]* Hmm. *[She continues walking. He tries all he can to delay her and talk to him.]*
PA BEN:	Why you greet me so cold?
MAMA:	A tired.
PA BEN:	You went out?
MAMA:	Hmm.
PA BEN:	A was wondering what happen to you. Me know is not like you to make dark catch you on the road.
MAMA:	The old bus broke down.
PA BEN:	The man who name that bus name it right. 'Surprise'. You surprise when it carry you home. Anyway you reach. You going out tomorrow?
MAMA:	A might.
PA BEN:	Outside of the district or what?
MAMA:	*[Angrily]* What you want?
PA BEN:	You have to be so short with me?
MAMA:	A say A tired.
PA BEN:	Anyway, if you going, let me know, nuh?
MAMA:	Hmm. *[She storms off.]*
PA BEN:	Somehow I going to have to detain her here tomorrow, play sick or something. *[As he goes into his house.]*

Act Two

Scene Four

Len is afraid of gossip & the spreading of rumours so he disguises himself.

16

[As the lights go down on the storyteller's area, they come up on LEN's living space. 'Beat'. LEN enters dressed in a straw hat, oversized dark glasses, outrageous red pants, and a vile sports jacket over an out-of-tune plaid shirt. He carries his briefcase and some flowers along with some bush. He locks the door behind him and charges towards the coffee table, where he rests briefcase, flowers and bush, then takes off dark glasses, straw hat and jacket, resting them on the chair behind the coffee table. He opens the briefcase and takes out two candles, then reaches behind him for the candle holders, sets the candles in, lights them and sets them down rather ceremoniously on the coffee table. Into his briefcase again for a list of instructions, he reads it quickly, then picks up the flowers and the bush. He starts an incantation, waving the flowers over his head, the bush round his waist.]

LEN: Protect her, protect her from the forces of evil!
                Search mi heart, hug me close, dead and wake,
                hug me close! *[He stops abruptly, finds a vase on the
                bookshelf, sticks the flowers in and places them on the
                coffee table. From his briefcase he takes out a vial and
                sprinkles a powdery substance in the four corners of the
                room, tossing it over his head. As he sprinkles, he cleans.
                The whole thing has to go at a terrific pace. Done with
                that, he digs into the briefcase and comes out with a
                pair of panties and a tape measure. A little unsure how
                to proceed, he goes to the telephone and dials. Before he
                completes the dialling, he panics, hangs up, returns to
                the chair, picks up dark glasses, hat and jacket and very
                quickly dresses himself. In fact, he is dialling and putting
                on his jacket at the same time.]*

LEN: *[In a fake accent]* Ah, Mother Rachael. Yes, the
                gentleman who was in to see you this morning.
                No. No, not the politician, the tall dark gentleman
                with the straw hat and the dark glasses … Yes. Oh
                very well, I got everything, including the oil of
                deliverance. There is just one little problem, the
                undergarment, does it go at the head of the table
                or … Ah, I see … Fine. Thank you. Good spirits to
                you as well!

[He hangs up, removes dark glasses, straw hat and jacket, then puts the tape measure at the head of the table, and places the panties on his head. Not

turning, he sort of reverses, walking as if he has a crick neck. He sprinkles the oil of deliverance in the corners of the room.]

Oil of deliverance. *[He does a little dance.]* Oil of deliverance. *[Dances.]* Oil of deliverance. *[Dances.]*

[A knocking is heard from off; LEN is visibly startled, panics in fact.]

Is that you, Lois?

LOIS: Your key is in the door.

LEN: Coming.

[Madly he attempts to stuff the things back in the briefcase, attempting at the same time to tidy up. A lot of business can be developed for this scene because as we will later discover that Mother Rachael is a fraud, so her potions for protection and deliverance can be as farcical as possible. LEN goes to the door, forgetting to remove the candles and one or two other items. He remembers the panties when he is halfway through opening the door. He snatches them off, puts them in his pocket, then opens the door fully. LOIS enters and goes directly to the table Down Right. LEN follows beside her.]

LOIS: Why you smiling so?

LEN: Smiling so? *[Still using the fake accent.]*

LOIS: What you been up to?

LEN: Been up to? Nothing. *[He reverts to his normal speech.]*

LOIS: Must you repeat everything I say?

LEN: Everything you say. I wasn't, was I? *[He checks behind him to discover the candles and whatever other items he has forgotten to clear. He somehow manages to get rid of them without LOIS seeing.]*

LOIS: What are you doing home anyway? Aren't you working today?

LEN: I just popped in to see how you were.

LOIS: I'm okay.

LEN: But you didn't look too good this morning.

LOIS: I'm fine.

LEN: But you look so pale, out of sorts, as if something's bothering you.

LOIS: Nothing.

LEN: You tossed and turned all night last night, won't tell you where you kicked me. *[Perspiring, yet relieved that the space is now clear. He goes for a handkerchief to mop his face, but the red panties come out. He is halfway through mopping his face when he realises. Quickly he pushes them away in his pocket.]* Ha, ha! What's the

	matter?
Lois:	Nothing, Len.
Len:	No pains, aches, dizziness?
Lois:	I'm having a bit of a headache.
Len:	Headache? When did it start?
Lois:	A day or so now.
Len:	That's all right. *[Catches himself.]* Anyway, sit down, I'll get you something. *[He puts her in the seat directly opposite to the flowers.]*
Lois:	What's the … Who brought these? *[The flowers.]*
Len:	Oh, I thought they'd cheer you up, my love. *[She looks at him in utter amazement.]* Why not, you are always accusing me that …
Lois:	Something terrible has happened.
Len:	No, it won't. Whatever you do, think positive.
Lois:	What's that you say?
Len:	Oh it was nothing, my love. To bring you some flowers. I said to myself *[he takes the flowers from the vase, and in the moment that Lois looks away, he repeats the business with the flowers over his head]*, what can I do to surprise her? So aren't you going to thank me? Give me a kiss.
Lois:	You are behaving most odd. Out with it. What have you been up to?
Len:	Not a thing.
Lois:	You are hiding something from me.
Len:	Goodness gracious, no. Wait till I really surprise you. Close your eyes. *[As he goes directly behind her.]*
Lois:	What are you up to?
Len:	Trust me.
Lois:	You know I don't.
Len:	Just this once, close your eyes, please.
Lois:	Len!
Len:	Please! *[She does.]* And no peeping. *[He makes the sign of the cross over the amulet which he takes from his pocket, pushing back the panties. He puts the amulet around her neck.]* There you are.
Lois:	Len!
Len:	Just a little something to restore your spirits. You look beautiful. Absolutely smashing! Promise me you will wear it always. *[He kisses her passionately on the mouth.]*

Irony:
religious
allusion

LOIS:	Wow! Okay, now give me the bad news.
LEN:	You'll have to understand what happened to me today.
LOIS:	I'll try.
LEN:	I was on my way to work this morning, and like Saul going to Damascus …
LOIS:	You were struck by a great light.
LEN:	As if in a vision, I had a stunning revelation.
LOIS:	The Virgin Mary is with child again.
LEN:	No, no, no. [*Searching in his pocket for another of his potions. Desperately he goes for his briefcase, sits himself down on the bar stool, the lid of the briefcase serving as a sort of mask as he digs around till he finds what he is looking for. While searching he continues his speech.*] All my life I've worked, slaved, buried myself. To what end? To no purpose. I was miserable. [*He finds the potion and hides it behind him. He puts the briefcase away again, and walks behind the chairs to Lois.*] From now on I am turning over a new leaf. In fact I am throwing away the books, getting a new lease on life. I am. Yes, I am unleashing myself on the pleasure spots of the world. I am going to freak out. [*He gets her up and leads her into a dance, a mixture of quickstep and tango. On each natural break in the dance, he sprinkles the potion behind her back.*] Yeah, drop out. [*He sits her down again, then goes directly behind her, and the action and the words should be so synchronised that as he touches her on the left shoulder, she automatically looks in that direction while he sprinkles the potion to her right.*] It all came to me in a flash, and since morning I've been making decisions right, left, and centre. One major decision is … Wait for it. [*His body language changes. He is trying to be very sexy. He goes to her, caresses, kisses her on the neck.*] Come, let's go upstairs. [*She is bemused. LEN pulls her up; she collects her bag, then he guides her in front of him, gently pushing her off.*]
LOIS:	I read somewhere that the world was coming to an end today. I think it has.

[*LEN removes the panties from his right pocket and twirls them around, a look of relief, pleasure, and accomplishment on his face, as the lights fade.*]

Act Two

Scene Five

17

[As the lights go down on the previous scene, they come up again almost immediately on the lower area. MAMA enters Down Left and calls across to GEORGE who we can imagine standing at his gate.]

MAMA:	Missa Mac. Missa Mac.
GEORGE:	Oh Miss G, how are you?
MAMA:	Right here, how you?
GEORGE:	Well, not too badly. I would invite you in, but the doctor's inside.
MAMA:	Somebody sick?
GEORGE:	Miss Margaret.
MAMA:	On top a everything else? Don't say that.
GEORGE:	Yes, last night one of my workmen phone her up, threaten to kill me if I don't pay him his doggone money.
MAMA:	Say what?
GEORGE:	Yes, so she is badly shook up, as you can imagine.
MAMA:	Lord, yes. You don't deserve this.
GEORGE:	The doctor trying to calm her down. Have her under sedation.
MAMA:	Poor little thing. Help her, oh Lord, help her!
GEORGE:	Imagine, the same workman who I have been helping to put bread in his mouth.
MAMA:	Bite the hand that feed them. The whole world gone mad.
GEORGE:	It's been a rough couple o' days. I could tell you. Sometimes I just feel as if I could throw in the towel.
MAMA:	No. Keep fighting, you hear what I tell you.
GEORGE:	Yes, Miss G.
MAMA:	I saw Len and I put in a word on your behalf.
GEORGE:	Thank you, Miss G.
MAMA:	Some good news soon come your way. In fact everything woulda been all right already if it wasn't for that. … Lawd! *[Beating her breast.]*
GEORGE:	What's the problem, Miss G?
MAMA:	A little obstacle in mi way.
GEORGE:	What obstacle?
MAMA:	It sorta private, but anyway the world have to know. Is the woman him married to.

GEORGE:	Lois, what about her?
MAMA:	She is a distress to me, you see, Missa Mac? But I know her number. She won't know what hit her when I finish with her. Len willing to help, but …
GEORGE:	And she said no?
MAMA:	She have him under influence.
GEORGE:	Lois?
MAMA:	She control him. Him mind don't belongs to him.
GEORGE:	Tell me more.
MAMA:	Leave it to me.
GEORGE:	No, I need to know all the details.
MAMA:	In a day or two everything will come through for you and Miss Margaret. You just have to trust me.
GEORGE:	You certain of your facts?
MAMA:	As certain as the night follows day *[confidentially]*, but you didn' hear nutten from me.
GEORGE:	No, no.
MAMA:	Just leave everything to me. A goin' now and tell Miss Margaret say the Lord is on her side.
GEORGE:	I'll do that.
MAMA:	And cheer up. Things goin' to be all right. *[As she leaves, boldly and positively]* You hear what A tell you.
GEORGE:	Take care, and thanks.

[GEORGE watches her go for a moment, then he too leaves the lower area.]

Act Two

Scene Six

[As the lights go down on the previous scene there is a knocking at the door.   **18** ✓
Lois answers.]

LOIS:	Hi, George, Len's not here, I'm afraid. *[George barges through past her.]* Was he expecting you?
GEORGE:	Don't ask me no questions, bitch!
LOIS:	I beg your pardon!
GEORGE:	Beg pardon? After I protect you that's the way you try and pay me back, by screwing me up!
LOIS:	What the hell is going on?
GEORGE:	Don't play the innocent with me. Your mother-in-law tell me how you set your husband against me.
LOIS:	What? Me? She said what?
GEORGE:	But I mean to get what I want, you see, and I'll expose you to get it.
LOIS:	No George, it's a damn lie. I'd have nothing to gain by …
GEORGE:	You have reason enough to hate my guts.
LOIS:	But more reason to protect you. What could I say to Len?
GEORGE:	I don't know what lie you cook up; anyway I didn't come here to talk to you. Your husband say the deal is off. When he comes, we reopen negotiations.
LOIS:	*[Imploringly]* George! *[She touches him. He pulls away.]*
GEORGE:	Don't even bother to try, baby.
LOIS:	You son of a bitch! *[She goes to the telephone and dials.]* Dr Tomlinson, please. Has he left for the day? Thank you.
LEN:	*[Entering]* Hi yah, beautiful, it's the new me. I got some good news. I called London today. *[She makes him aware of George who is sitting on the sofa.]* Hi ya, George.
GEORGE:	Hi, man.
LEN:	My secretary gave you a message, didn't she?
GEORGE:	Yeah, I got the message.
LEN:	I'm sorry things didn't work out.
GEORGE:	That's all right, they will.
LEN:	Good.
GEORGE:	Sit down.

63

2.6

LEN:	I beg your pardon.
GEORGE:	I am reopening negotiations.
LOIS:	Len.
LEN:	Yes.
LOIS:	George has something to tell you.

✓ 19
Flasback –
Episode 2

[LEN moves Upstage and freezes. LOIS turns her back to the audience, puts on a jacket which suggests her bank uniform, then freezes. In the meantime GEORGE gets up and goes across to the desk Down Right. He sits, picks up the phone and dials just one number.]

GEORGE:	Five minutes ago I asked Miss Stuart to come in, where is she? And no calls through to me till I tell you.

Lois Stuart

[LOIS breaks the freeze and enters GEORGE's office. LEN has turned his back on the action.]

LOIS:	You wanted to see me, Sir?
GEORGE:	What took you so long?
LOIS:	I only just got the message.
GEORGE:	Oh. Have a look at this. *[Hands her bank cards.]* You handle those accounts, don't you?
LOIS:	Well, yes, sir.
GEORGE:	I was hoping you could throw some light on the matter.
LOIS:	I don't know, sir.
GEORGE:	Miss Stuart, you must know. The lady who the account belongs to was in to see me this morning. She says she's been living in England for the last eight years. That last withdrawal was made on the eighteenth of this month, two days before she left England.
LOIS:	There has to be some mistake.
GEORGE:	I would say it's more than that.
LOIS:	I'll go and check the ledger.
GEORGE:	Don't waste my time. *[Hiss.]* Tell you what, let me get the police in on this. *[He picks up the phone.]*
LOIS:	Sir! *[Pause.]*
GEORGE:	Yes, Miss Stuart? You want the cops in on it or not? *[Pause.]*
LOIS:	No, sir. *[He hangs up after another pause.]*
GEORGE:	I thought I knew every trick in the book, but this is a new one on me. I take my hat off to you. When I found out what you were up to, I had a choice: call the cops, or do what anybody in my position

	would do – protect his staff. As luck would have it, the customer we are dealing with wasn't too smart. I managed to sort it out with her; inflation, devaluation, bank charges, that sort of thing. Learn one thing in this life: you can sell anything to people, so long as you package it right! She left happy. Naturally my curiosity was aroused, so I did a little digging.
LOIS:	I can explain.
GEORGE:	You been playing this game for quite a little while, little bit here, little bit there.
LOIS:	Most of it's been repaid, Sir, I only …
GEORGE:	The deed is done, my dear: now we must cover your tracks. Damn bad luck on your part. If the woman had kept her tail in England you would have got away with it. Anyway, in future when you are a bit strapped for cash, check with me, I am sure we can come to some arrangement. *[He touches her.]*
LOIS:	Thank you, sir, but …
GEORGE:	I know how you girls like to dress up, show off on the fellows. *[He is playing with her blouse.]*
LOIS:	The money wasn't for me …
GEORGE:	No?
LOIS:	There's this friend …
GEORGE:	Boyfriend, eh, put you up to it?
LOIS:	You don't understand, sir. He doesn't know. He's at university, and we have this arrangement; I would work and pay his way, and later …
GEORGE:	You send him away on a scholarship. Good.
LOIS:	But since then my father died, and me being the eldest, all the responsibility for the younger ones fell on me. You won't say anything to anyone, will you, Sir? *[She cries.]*
GEORGE:	This is strictly between us.
LOIS:	*[Crying]* I'll pay it all back.
GEORGE:	What you crying for? Come, come. On to brighter things, like how you planning to thank me. Tell you what, to show good faith, proof that I won't go back on my word, it'll be my pleasure to drop my signature right here on this card, then nobody can touch you, and who is going to accuse me?

	I am a citizen above suspicion. But later for that. *[He walks away from her and sits on the sofa.]* Why am I sticking my neck out for you? Two reasons. You are one of the first black girls that the bank employ. Think what it would do for your race if the news was to get out; and secondly, as a man I couldn't sit back and see an attractive girl like you go to waste in some dirty prison, just for a few dollars. No way. Such a nice body, pretty face like that. Come here.
Lois:	Please, Mr McFarlane. No!
George:	Call me George. *[As he goes towards her and touches her again.]*
Lois:	Please, Sir, no!
George:	I like you for a long time now.
Lois:	No!
George:	I bet you could feel me looking at you.
Lois:	No! *[As he tries to kiss her]* No! *[She pushes him away.]*
George:	Wait a minute, baby, I am not going to wrestle with you at all. Take your time, think it over. After all the stress you owe it to yourself to have a little relaxation. *[He sits on the sofa.]* The choice is yours, for I can easily put this matter back on a strictly business basis. Come here.

✓ 20

[She starts removing her jacket. She takes one tentative step towards George, then another. On the third she breaks down crying and runs away from him towards the entrance to the area upstairs. Len runs after her, embraces and consoles her. George is still sitting on the sofa. Lois is crying uncontrollably.]

Love

Len:	It's okay, it's okay.
Lois:	Oh, Len, I am so sorry. I have ruined everything.
Len:	It's okay, sweetheart, we are in this together now.
Lois:	I'll go away. I'll do anything.
George:	Touching scene.
Lois:	Let me go upstairs. I have this splitting headache.
Len:	Yes, go and lie down. *[He walks with her to the door.]* You son of a bitch! *[To George]*
George:	*[Showing the withdrawal slip]* The withdrawal slip your wife signed to defraud the bank. Kept a copy as a little souvenir. Never know when these things will come in handy. *[Len takes it.]* Tear that up, the original's at home.
Len:	*[Looking at it]* This is no longer valid in a court of law.
George:	I know that, but I can use it to damage you, man.

A man in your position can't afford a scandal. This
is a small town, word travels fast, plus you never
know how I will twist the story when I release it.
It could even involve you. Who is going to believe
you never knew what she was up to? The story
might even get around that you put her up to it.

risk spreading rumours

21 ✓

[LEN *grabs him by the collar. Immediately there is an urgent knocking at the
door.* LEN *releases* GEORGE.]

LEN: Come in. [PA BEN *enters. He is very agitated.*] Pa
                Ben!
PA BEN: Missa Lenny. [*He sees* GEORGE] All well. All well.
GEORGE: Fine.
PA BEN: Cry excuse, beg pardon, forgive mi manners. A can
                talk to you in private?
LEN: Yes, of course. [*They move down left away from*
                GEORGE.] Is it about Mama?
PA BEN: No, Missa Lenny, is about Mother Rachael.
LEN: What about her?
PA BEN: She is a fraud!
LEN: What! Where'd you get this?
PA BEN: Reliable sources. She is an impostor, a bogus.
LEN: Oh no! Jesus! You know anybody else?
PA BEN: Is too late for that. Talk to your mother. Is yuh last
                chance. Pray God you not too late.
LEN: We're right back where we started, going around in
                circles.
PA BEN: How is Miss Lois? Any sign of anything?
LEN: No. Well, she had a headache just now.
PA BEN: Headache? Oh my God! Negotiate with your
                Mama. In another couple of hours Miss Lois could
                be of no use to herself.
LOIS: [*Calling from off*] Len, Len.
LEN: Excuse me. [*He goes off to her. There is a pause.* PA BEN
                in his nervousness wanders around the space.]
PA BEN: [*To* GEORGE] All well. All well.
GEORGE: All well.
PA BEN: Aye. [LEN *returns nervously to the drinks table and is
                getting some aspirins.*] Tablets is of no use if…
LEN: It's just an ordinary headache.
PA BEN: You think. You can't take any chances at this the
                eleventh hour. Him is your only hope. [*Pointing to*
                GEORGE.]

LEN:	*[Thinks momentarily.]* You know you right. Old man, you are a genius, absolute genius.
PA BEN:	But I been telling you that all the time.
LEN:	Go find Mama and bring her back here. Whatever you do, don't come back without her.
PA BEN:	Oh, I aint go fail you, but it going be hard.
LEN:	All right.
PA BEN:	All right. *[He is going when he stops and turns.]* Hey, now listen, you have to tell Miss Lois everything.
LEN:	Yes, yes, yes.
PA BEN:	Thank God you see the light.
LEN:	Hurry.
PA BEN:	All right. Praise God. I hope we not too late. *[He goes.]*
LEN:	*[To GEORGE]* I'll be a little while. While you are waiting, you might like something to read.
GEORGE:	I'm fine.
LEN:	I insist. After all it's your life story. *[LEN pushes the dossier at GEORGE. He takes it rather tentatively. LEN goes off with the aspirin to LOIS.]*
PA BEN:	*[Appears on the lower level]* Quick as a flash I was on mi way, all the time mi brain going tick tick, like a clock, trying to think up a story to get Miss Aggy to come back with me, but you know I am a storyteller. Before the hour hand had gone around once in mi mind, I knew what I was going to tell her, and A knew she would go back to town with me.
GEORGE:	Oh shit! *[Reading the dossier.]*
PA BEN:	More or less. *[He travels, from Stage Right to Stage Left going off, to reappear immediately with MAMA in tow.]* In a flash we was heading back to town on the ol' country bus 'Surprise'. A pray for it to surprise me today and nuh bruck down. The one question A wanted to ask Miss Aggy, A couldn't ask, but A had a feeling I would find out soon enough. Lawd, A hope we not too late. If we is, today going be the day. *[They go off as Len appears in his area.]*
LEN:	Not a very pretty picture, is it? Then again, it's not the whole story. There's still a little surprise package I have for you.
GEORGE:	Hang on to this, I'll go home and get the original,

	then we can forget the whole thing.
LEN:	Sit your ass down. There are two signatures on this, yours and my wife's. It'll be hard to prove who signed first.
GEORGE:	I said I was willing to forget it, man.
LEN:	Forget! How many times did you yourself use this same method to defraud the bank?
GEORGE:	What?
LEN:	You heard me. You knew all the tricks but one. Lois taught you something new, didn't she? In this little surprise package that I promised you, twenty photostat copies of withdrawal slips all signed by you, and some innocent bank clerk. In a couple of cases yours is the sole signature. All within the last seven years, therefore valid in law. It could be ten years in jail or more. The Director of Public Prosecutions should find this very interesting. *[As he goes to the telephone.]*
GEORGE:	Wait a minute, man.
LEN:	Ten chances to one, you'll get buggered the first night in prison. Then again there's your family to consider. Margaret is principal shareholder in A.B.C., so is your mother.
GEORGE:	They didn't know. Leave them out.
LEN:	Conspiracy to defraud. Jail again. It's going to be a full house!
GEORGE:	Jesus Christ, man, if you want me to beg, I will beg. I beg you, I'll do anything. Please, I just couldn't face it. Have a heart. What do you want me to do, clean your shoes? *[As he goes on his knees in front of LEN.)*
LEN:	Okay. When my mother comes, you will tell her how you took her for a ride.
GEORGE:	Whatever you say.
LEN:	Good. Not just about the house now.
GEORGE:	What else is there?
LEN:	Among other things, Cassava Nova. Rings a bell? At Munro, by the old bell tower.
GEORGE:	*[Pause]* You?
LEN:	Tell her what happened that night, George, and the events leading up to it. Leave nothing out. *[Pause.]*
GEORGE:	And after that, what you going to do with me?

[handwritten margin notes:]
Len is driven by malice & the desire for revenge

profanity in comparison to Len's schoolboy servitude

Len is not merciless & forgiving

Len:	This could still go to the Director of Public Prosecutions. It's a chance you'll have to take.

[There is a knocking at the door. Lois enters from the direction of the bedroom. Len opens the door. Pa Ben enters, and points to Mama behind him. Mama comes on almost immediately.]

	Hello, Mama.
Mama:	*[Very surprised to see him.]* Len! *[To Pa Ben]* But how come you tell me …?
Len:	We need to talk to you, Mama. *[Mama sees Lois.]*
Mama:	*[To Pa Ben]* You trick me. *[Seeing George]* Missa Mac?
George:	Miss G.
Mama:	What dis mean?

[The lights go down on all but the Storyteller's area.]

Pa Ben:	You see dat boy make me go home and bring him Ma back, I thinking he want to settle up with Mongoose in front of her. But no, Missa Lenny start to replay the story of his youth in the days when Mama drumbeat Miss Margaret so much in him head. Miss Margaret; Advancement; Advancement; till him gone like a fool write love-letter to the girl, and that's when the perpendicular meet the contuberance, which in lay the conbrucksion.

[During Pa Ben's speech to the audience, George goes off; so does Len. Mama and Lois stand with their backs to the audience. As Pa Ben finishes his speech he also faces upstage. At the same time Margaret comes on with a letter in her hand. She is calling out for George.]

Margaret:	Georgie! Georgie! Georgie! *[George, wearing his school cap, enters behind her as she is calling. He surprises her, tries to hold and kiss her.]* No Georgie, look what that fellow sent me.
George:	What! *[He takes the letter and shoves it into his pocket, then continues slobbering over Margaret.]*
Margaret:	It's a love-letter.
George:	Love-letter? *[He breaks his hold on her and gets the letter from his pocket.]*
Margaret:	That black, ugly, little big-lipped ugly …
George:	You mean Tomlinson, the school mascot? *[He starts to read.]* 'I love you with a love that knows no boundary.'

(handwritten notes in margins:) ✓ 22 Climax of the play begins. Flashback – Episode 3. Margaret means pearl

70

MARGARET:	Not aloud. Give it back. *[As she tries to take it back.]*
GEORGE:	'With a passion that leaves me breathless.' What! 'Helen of Troy, Cleopatra, Margaret, the fairest of them all. Princess, I call out your name and the echoes ring like cathedral bells summoning me to worship at thy feet. Oh goddess!' Shit! *[He gives her back the letter. They sit.]* Your daddy seen this?
MARGARET:	He'd have a heart attack. God knows he's a generous man, but he expects those people to know their place. He'd expel the boy …
GEORGE:	I'd say right away.
MARGARET:	'Cept daddy would refuse to believe it's entirely the boy's doing.
GEORGE:	So who?
MARGARET:	Well, the boy's got a rather ignorant unfortunate dragon of a mother, she must have put him up to it, always bowing and scraping, wheedling her way into father's favour. A real little pest.
GEORGE:	But it's the boy who wrote the letter. He should have more sense than that. We have to put him in his place. This has to go up on the school notice-board. *[He starts to go.* MARGARET *runs and stops him.]*
MARGARET:	Out of the question, Georgie. Think of my reputation.

[As she tries desperately to get the letter.]

GEORGE:	Remain silent and see what happens. Next thing you know the rumour gets out with all the nasty innuendoes. We have to nip this in the bud.
MARGARET:	No, Georgie, please.
GEORGE:	On second thoughts, you know *[he gives her the letter with a flourish]* pinning that on the notice board is no big thing, it'll be a little laugh. In a couple of days it's blown over and done with. No. We need something that lover-boy will never forget as long as he lives.
MARGARET:	*[who has been stuffing the letter in her shoe]* Like what, Georgie?
GEORGE:	You have to reply to the letter.
MARGARET:	You out of your mind Georgie?
GEORGE:	I'll compile the letter. You will tell him you received his letter, and you need to see him, urgent. Tonight in fact. He must meet you after

rumours

lights-out down by the old fort, next to the cannon. Me and the other boys will be waiting for him. *[As he removes his belt.]*

MARGARET: Oh, it'll be ever such good sport, eh, Georgie?

GEORGE: And you don't know what I am coming up with yet.

[They go off together in high spirits. GEORGE shouts from off, 'Lights out'. In the darkness the actors on stage stack the three chairs that make up the sofa, and the coffee table Upstage. In the darkness LEN screams, terrible and long. A spotlight picks him up as he appears in the auditorium. A pillow case has been tied over his head, his hands are tied in front of him, his trousers are about his ankles. His screaming, mixed with his sobbing, continues over the taunts of his attackers. LEN runs, trying to find his way.]

GEORGE: That'll teach you, lover-boy! That'll teach you. Next time we cut it off. This was just a rehearsal. Next time it's for real, so let this be a lesson to you, lover-boy. You cassava-nova you. *[He laughs.]* Cassava-nova, yeah, cassava-nova! Breathe a word of this to anybody and you know what you will get, you hear me, boy. Don't forget. *[GEORGE picks up a couple of imaginary stones and throws them after LEN. The action freezes momentarily. GEORGE removes his red school cap, gives it to MARGARET, who takes it and exit Up Left. The lights come up. LEN returns to the stage, dressed as he was before the flashback.]*

MAMA: *[Spinning and charging GEORGE with her handbag]* You wicked evil wretch!

GEORGE: What the …

LEN: Mama! *[Going after her.]*

MAMA: A have to wash mi hand in him blood. *[PA BEN and LEN try to restrain her.]* Let me go! Make A kill him!

LEN: All right, Mama.

PA BEN: Miss G.

[GEORGE escapes through the Up Right door.]

MAMA: I have to kill him! *[They take away the handbag.]* No, don't make me go to mi grave with mi soul in torment, Lawd, mi spirit in bondage. I have to atone for mi sins. I have to cleanse mi soul. Oh Len, how I going to sleep tonight? How I will sleep ever again? Oh Len, Len, forgive me, please, forgive me.

LEN: Mama, the story is not finished yet.

MAMA:	No. I don't want to hear any more.
LEN:	I ran away from school that night and stayed away for a week.
MAMA:	But you didn't come home?
LEN:	No, I didn't.
MAMA:	Where you went?
LEN:	A good Samaritan and his daughter took care of me till I could go back to school.
MAMA:	Who are these people? They living?
LEN:	Her father is dead, Mama.
MAMA:	Heaven rest his soul! I have to find the daughter to thank her.
LEN:	I married her, Mama. *[Pause.]* She was good to me, and I love her.

[MAMA looks at LOIS, and as if hit by a bullet she immediately begins to lose control of mind and body. She tries to escape Down Left.]

MAMA:	Help me, oh Lord! Give me the strength to do what I have to do before the sun go down! *[They all four look at the setting sun.]* Miss Lois, I am not begging forgiveness. Just take care of mi son, is all I ask.
LOIS:	Miss Aggy!
MAMA:	Oh daughter! Child! *[They hug each other.]* The time is going. Pa Ben? *[As she goes to him.]*
PA BEN:	Yes, Miss Aggy.
MAMA:	A could never have had a better friend, you know.
PA BEN:	No. I let you down.
MAMA:	No, you tried with me. I took mi chances. I knew the consequences. I do it to miself.
PA BEN:	Yes, no, Miss Aggy. *[Deeply overcome with emotion.]*
MAMA:	Len, son, I am a foolish old woman.
LEN:	No, Mama.
MAMA:	Take care o' Miss Lois and find a little happiness for yourself. You hear me.
LEN:	Yes, Mama. I love you, Mama.
MAMA:	Aye, mi son, let me go. I don't want night to catch me on the road. *[She is going.]* It is going to be a long night.
LOIS:	*[Barring the door.]* 'The Lord is my shepherd.'
MAMA:	Stop it. *[Turning fast.]*
LOIS:	'I shall not want.'
MAMA:	No. No, don't do it. Don't endanger yourself. Pa

73

	Ben, warn her, tell her.
Pa Ben:	Miss Lois!
Lois:	I know the risks.
Mama:	No. Not for me, Miss Lois.
Pa Ben:	If you willing for a fight, I willing to fight with you.
Mama:	Not for me. Len!
Len:	We need you, Mama.

[As Mama tries to escape they encircle her. Their hands come together and Mama is trapped in the circle.]

Mama:	No, no, don't do this to yourselves. No, no!
Pa Ben, Len, Lois:	[Break into the chant] Omia n Twi. Mia Kuru. Omia n ani.

[Mama screams, wrenched with pain, as the prayer for her deliverance from the evil spirits continues.]

Pa Ben:	Omia n Twi. Mia Kuru. Omia n ani.

[After some time Pa Ben leaves the circle and goes towards the audience.]

religious reference

Love & the black community

The theme of Love

All night long we pray. We pray for strength in this the vigil of the long night. We bind ourselves together with strength and trust and confidence, and there was no doubt between us, no enmity in our hearts, for we knew that the one force that could counteract all evil was there, and that force was love.

[All during the above speech Len and Lois hold on to Mama as they repeat the twenty-third psalm. There is a note of real urgency and desperation in the prayer. The struggle goes on for a little while longer, then it quietens, and in the gentlest voice Mama sings 'Omia n Twi'. There is a silence as the circle is bathed with a warm rich light.]

lighting (as an essential production element)

He is inviting us to cry (he is commenting on the action trying to influence our responses)

Mama:	My children, my children. [As she hugs Len and Lois.]
Pa Ben:	[Sitting in his chair] A tell you, every time A see the three of them together as a family, the feeling just well up inside, and the eye water … [He starts to cry in his joyfulness. He gets up, overcome with emotion, and goes towards his little house. He stops by the doorway, then he turns, looks at the family, and smiles.] All well. [The lights go down slowly.]

Harmony & Redemption

Study Notes

Introduction to the study notes

When we study a play we are reading words which were written to be performed. In order to pay proper attention to the script, we need to be aware of the many non-verbal elements involved in the staging of it. The set, the costumes, the lighting and the audience response, all contribute significantly to our experience in the theatre. The presence of actors is crucially important. Who, physically, are the people speaking these words? With what timing, in what manner, at what volume, might the words be delivered? At this particular moment, what does this person want? What is the body language saying? Is there meaning in the shifting pattern of groups on stage? What does the audience see and hear?

In his notes on 'The Setting', 'Furniture', 'Costumes' and in stage directions, Rhone gives many indications of how the piece might be presented. He directed productions of *Old Story Time* before the play was published, and the published script is often describing performance details he has seen to work – such as the mime sequence of 'the Hi Poshers riding into the school yard in them shiny new buggies with the big black stallions in harness' (page 42). '*The transition happens smoothly and there is no break in the action*' (page 42). The stage directions are sometimes telling the actor what the playwright wants the dialogue to communicate: as in 'GEORGE: Len Tomlinson? Oh yeah. [*He most decidedly has not remembered LEN.*]' (page 37) They may offer detailed instructions on how to '*change the set around*' with the audience watching, a manoeuvre completed '*in a half light*' (page 30). Lighting is an essential production element: at the very beginning, for example, in the darkness we hear the actors singing a folk song and '*we see the glow of Pa Ben's lantern*' (page 10). At the end of the play '*the circle is bathed with a warm rich light*' (page 78).

First performed in April 1979, *Old Story Time* continues to please and instruct various audiences. It is set in Jamaica between the 1940s and the 1970s, when there was still widespread discrimination on the grounds of colour, which is one of the play's main concerns. It also explores other aspects of Jamaican life, including Jamaicans' relationship with Christianity and obeah, and makes use of various elements in Jamaica's rich folklore.

The opening moments establish a storytelling atmosphere and introduce the main storyteller, Pa Ben. An early stage direction reads: '[*he re-enacts the memory.*]' *Old Story Time* is partly told, and partly enacted/re-enacted: it flexibly combines the two approaches. The enactment that follows the initial sequence continues the story Pa Ben has begun to tell. Act Two opens similarly, with similar effect.

The play begins with Pa Ben – 'Old Story Time' – and it ends with him, 'All well'. All's well that ends well. Act One develops steadily. Len is taken from boy to man. We see conflict about Lois developing between Miss Aggy and Len. We are introduced to the villain, George, and are intrigued by his unexplained relationship to Lois. The pace of the drama quickens in Act Two as complications multiply. Act One ends with an expression of hatred. Act Two ends in harmony and redemption.

These notes assume that you have read and are re-reading the play. The section on **Plot Development**, which follows the sequence of the script, seeks to test and reinforce your understanding of detail. **People, Values and Social Context** discusses issues raised in the work. **Performance and the Playwright's Craft** examines how Rhone has shaped and focused his material.

Plot Development

Summaries, notes and questions

wk. 1/4
✓

The storytelling atmosphere is established: darkness; a quiet folk song; the glow of a lantern. Over the song, Pa Ben announces 'Old Story Time', summoning the audience – not just the actors who will assemble, but also the people seated in the auditorium waiting for the play to begin. The effect is strengthened if, as the stage directions indicate, Pa Ben enters the auditorium, passing through the theatre audience on his way to the stage. What he says right after those first words – from 'Evening, one and all. Everybody hearty?' – is directed both at the actors who will constitute his audience on stage and at his audience in the auditorium. Although the script says '[*The actors respond* …]' it is not unusual for the auditorium audience to join the actors in 'Yes, Pa Ben'.

Then Pa Ben specifically addresses the people in the auditorium, reminding them of the comparatively comfortable conditions in which they will hear the story, in contrast to the storytelling contexts of his youth: conviviality and charm but 'no opportunity for us black people'. As the actors become his immediate audience on stage, Pa Ben locates himself in a tradition, invoking the memory of his father who was 'the chief Storyteller when him feel in the mood'.

The storyteller sometimes exaggerates. Pa Ben says he used to read by the light of fireflies in a bottle. He argues that living next door to some of the people in his story gives him 'first-hand knowledge'. He cheerfully asserts the storyteller's right to invent: 'What A don't know as a fact, A will make up as A go along.' White rum will assist him if necessary.

The performance of '*a very uptempo blues version of the folk song*' which the actors/villagers listen to 'bemused', serves to emphasise by contrast our engagement in an old-time story. In Rhone's productions, the group on stage go off by jumping sideways with feet together as in a children's game. Pa Ben, chanting 'Ol' Story Time', disappears inside his house, and the enactment of the story begins.

✔ 1 What reasons does Pa Ben give for saying, 'You people lucky'?

✔ 2 Why does someone say, 'Him don't have no liver'?

✔ ## 2 pages 8–11

Miss Aggy has returned from the market, tired, with a present for her friend, Pa Ben. She goes in search of her son, Len, whom she had expected to find studying. Len has gone off with his village friend Pearl, who says he is 'hoititoity'. Miss Aggy discovers them in the river, and she punishes Len, insisting that 'anything black nuh good'. She has identified for Len two strategies of 'advancement': education, and marriage to a light-skinned woman. She has picked out for him 'Miss Margaret, Reverend Greaves daughter, a nice brown girl with tall hair down to her back.'

✱ **Questions**

✔ 1 Identify two bits of evidence that Pa Ben and Miss Aggy are friends.

✔ 2 Identify two matters on which they seem to differ.

✔ 3 Find two bits of evidence that suggest that Miss Aggy is a very strict parent.

✔ 4 Give two of Miss Aggy's reasons for beating Len.

✔ ## 3 pages 11–13

After this enactment Pa Ben reappears as storyteller, both to comment on Miss Aggy's attitude, and to move us swiftly several years on. He mentions meeting Len with 'a pretty black girl', Lois, and agreeing not to tell Miss Aggy. Len goes away to England on a scholarship and communicates with Pa Ben through Lois, while Miss Aggy remains in the dark. Not hearing from her son, Miss Aggy begins to worry, but Pa Ben, having promised Len, does not tell her what he knows. Miss Aggy begins to wonder whether obeah is at work, whether 'somebody in the district burn a candle on [Len's] head.'

1 Why does Pa Ben say he is sure that nothing (untoward) has happened to Len?

2 Why does Pa Ben not tell Miss Aggy he has heard from Len?

3 What reasons does Miss Aggy give for thinking it possible that 'somebody in the district burn a candle on [Len's] head'?

4 pages 13–18

When Pearl, now broken down and pregnant, enquires about Len, Miss Aggy tells her a lie, claiming to have recently received a letter from him. Miss Aggy wonders whether Len has gone mad, perhaps from too much study.

An airmail letter arrives. Pa Ben and Miss Aggy are excited. There is money in the envelope: but the letter, which, at Miss Aggy's request, Pa Ben reads aloud, is very brief and formal. Miss Aggy is appalled by its neglect of courtesies. She becomes convinced that somebody or something is turning her son against her, that 'Evil forces [are] at work' (page 18). Realising that Pearl has overheard the letter and the subsequent conversation, Miss Aggy and Pa Ben rush off in pursuit of her to 'buy her silence'.

* **Questions**

1 Why does Miss Aggy tell Pearl a lie?

2 Why does Pearl look older than she is?

3 Why does Miss Aggy remove Pa Ben's hand when he rests it on her thigh?

4 Miss Aggy says: 'if me never did fight an' struggle with the one Mass Len, all now him would be knocking 'bout the district a turn wutliss like the rest a them.' Do you agree with her or not? Give reasons for your answer.

5 Why does Pa Ben ask Miss Aggy if 'Missa Lenny did intimate anything about Miss Margaret before him leave'?

6 What reasons does Pa Ben give for recommending that Miss Aggy attend Mass Zaccy's 'nine night' function?

7 Why does Pa Ben pour some of his drink on the ground?

8 Why does Pa Ben say, 'Thank you, brother Zaccy'?

8   Why does Pa Ben say, 'Thank you, brother Zaccy'?

9   Why does Len's letter make Miss Aggy think 'Them light candle 'pon him head'?

10 Why do Miss Aggy and Pa Ben *go chasing after Pearl*?

5   pages 18–21

Pa Ben writes, begging Len to make peace with his mother, and Len starts writing more frequently. Then one day Miss Aggy, bawling, tells Pa Ben she now knows who has set obeah on her son. It must be 'the gal in the picture' she has received from Len, a picture of him and his wife, a black woman. Recognising Lois, Pa Ben very nearly reveals his guilty knowledge. Miss Aggy tears the photograph in two, saying 'Me nuh want her beside mi son'. Pa Ben rebukes her, deeming her attitude 'ignorance'. The word offends Miss Aggy and she quarrels with Pa Ben.

For over a year she does not speak to him. But Pa Ben continues to be friendly, and finally she relents. Pa Ben – convinced that Miss Aggy is still 'carrying feelings' for Len's wife, Lois – guesses that only the chance that she might be wrong has kept Miss Aggy from going to the obeah man 'to go hit back at the girl', for 'Is a terrible thing when you go to the obeah man to seek vengeance, an' it turn roun' an' come back at you.'

Note
page 20: Kirrout – Stop it; get out (clear out).

Questions

1   Reporting that Miss Aggy was feeling better, Pa Ben says 'the colour come back into her cheeks'. How appropriate is the expression? What does it tell us about Pa Ben's education?

2   Pa Ben says that when he realised Len was in Africa, he fretted for him. What reasons does Pa Ben give for fretting? Is Pa Ben right to fret? What do the reasons he gives tell us about Pa Ben's education?

3   Why does Pa Ben call Africa 'the dark continent'?

4   Why does Pa Ben regard Len's return to England as 'deliverance'?

5   Why does Miss Aggy believe that the woman in the photograph

has set obeah on Len?

✓ 6 Having blurted out 'Miss Lois', how does Pa Ben persuade Miss Aggy that that is not what he said? What makes his stratagey work?

✓ 7 Why does Pa Ben tell Miss Aggy, 'Stop living in the past'?

✓ 8 Pa Ben says to Miss Aggy, 'before you … set evil forces at work to try an' hit back at the chile, consider the one chance you might be wrong, an' when you done consider that, consider the consequences.' What consequences does he refer to?

✓ 9 Why is Pa Ben surprised when Miss Aggy tells him 'Evening'?

✓ Wk. ²/₄ **6 pages 21–5**

Len returns, very formal in manner. Pa Ben is excited. Miss Aggy is overcome: 'Joy, Mass Len. Joy.' Pearl enters, pregnant again, more broken down than before. At the instigation of Miss Aggy, Len gives her some money, 'for the baby when it comes'.

Len is an economist with a Ph.D., not a medical doctor as Miss Aggy had assumed. On learning that the dress Len has brought her was selected by his wife, Miss Aggy pointedly puts it aside, reasserting her hostility to Lois. Miss Aggy tells Len of having invested in a house for him. She resists his concern that she should make her own home more modern and more comfortable. She takes up the matter of his marriage, insisting that Lois has put obeah on him.

✶ **Questions**

✓ 1 Why does Miss Aggy urge Len to give something to Pearl? What does her request tell us about the differing situations of Len and Pearl?

✓ 2 Look again at question 4 of section 4. Answer it again.

✓ 3 Pa Ben seems to think it more urgent that he get a few starapples for Len than receive the gift that Len has brought him. How does this detail affect your impression of Pa Ben?

✓ 4 Why does Miss Aggy think Len will cure her cough?

✓ 5 What does Miss Aggy mean by 'a true true doctor'?

✓ 6 What reasons does Miss Aggy give for preferring not to 'fix up' her place?

✓ ## 7 pages 25–29

To the singing of 'Change the house round' the set is speedily transformed into the home of Len and Lois.

There is tension in the air. Lois is complaining of sexual neglect. Miss Aggy arrives at the gate, calling 'Hold dog!', one of the ways in which she expresses animosity to Lois. On entering she is discourteous to Lois in various ways. Lois insults her in return.

Len reports that he has been investigating the arrangements about the house Miss Aggy 'paid down on' and that he does not have good news. He asks Miss Aggy to tell him how she got into the scheme.

✳ ### Questions

✓ 1 What is Lois complaining about? Indicate evidence in the script that supports your answer.

✓ 2 Why does Miss Aggy call 'Hold dog!'?

✓ 3 Identify two things Miss Aggy does or says which might cause offence to Lois.

✓ 4 Identify the moment when Lois hits back at Miss Aggy. Explain the nature of the insult.

✓ ## 8 pages 29–32

Miss Aggy's answer begins with an enactment. George McFarlane contacts her in the bank, advising investment in real estate as a hedge against inflation. George mentions the death of his father-in-law, Reverend Greaves, and Miss Aggy realises that George has married Miss Margaret.

In the present Miss Aggy explains that she has not heard from George McFarlane recently and he no longer works at the bank. Making offensive remarks again about her daughter-in-law, Miss Aggy leaves the home of Len and Lois.

Note

page 28: Topsy – a black slave girl in the novel *Uncle Tom's Cabin*, by Harriet Beecher Stowe.

Questions

1 What reasons does George give Miss Aggy for recommending that she 'pay down on a little house'?

2 Why has George befriended Miss Aggy?

3 Len tells Miss Aggy, 'I think I am beginning to understand, Mama.' What is he beginning to understand?

4 Why is Len embarrassed by Miss Aggy's story about the pigs?

5 Why does Miss Aggy ask if 'The dog tie'?

9 pages 32–4

George McFarlane comes to see Len Tomlinson. George and Lois recognise each other. Lois asks him to pretend that she and George have never met before. A telephone call from his business associate makes it clear that George is under great financial pressure.

Questions

1 When Lois says 'I mustn't complain', George says 'No. By the look of things, no.' What does he mean?

2 When Lois offers George a drink, he says 'The usual.' What does that seem to say about their relationship?

10 pages 34–40

Len, who works at the Development Bank, comes home to find George waiting to see him. Over drinks, the two move cautiously, with Len asking questions which George has anticipated about the viability of George's business, ABC Homes. George says he is convinced he has an enemy trying to destroy him. Having considered the figures supplied by George, Len tells him what his group might be willing to pay. Flabbergasted at the lowness of the offer, George changes tack, proposing now that Len take 'a piece o' [the] action', for personal gain. Len says he will think about it.

Len identifies George as a Munro old boy nicknamed 'Mongoose'. George evidently does not remember Len. George reminisces about the old school, deploring socialistic changes that have been taking place: the school is '[p]acked now with a bunch o' riff-raff scholarship winners'.

Hearing a noise outside, George draws his gun, and reveals himself to be 'a nervous wreck', fearful for himself and his family. Declining Len's invitation to supper, he mentions that he is married to Margaret, daughter of Reverend Greaves. Len asks if he remembers a boy at school called Blackie. George's memory is uncertain, but he tells a story about a boy whose mother visited him on Open Day with a basket on her head. When she missed her step, one of the totos from the basket rolled near the headmaster and the Chairman of the Board. Thereafter the boy was called 'Toto'.

The boy was Len, who now identifies himself, pretending to be amused. When George lamely enquires after Len's mother, Len mentions that George owes her money on the house deal. When Lois enters, George declines another drink and leaves, embarrassed.

After George's departure, Len laughs and laughs. Then in the final words before the intermission, he reveals to the audience a bitterness he has carefully concealed from George.

Note
page 37: 'Benedictus benedicat, per Jesum Christum dominum nostrum' – A Latin grace meaning: May the blessed one bless [the food and us], through Jesus Christ, our Lord.

Questions

1 When George tells Len he has a list of prospective purchasers willing to buy the houses at an escalated price, Len asks about the people who have bought houses already. George says, 'They pay the escalated price, or get their money back.' What is wrong with that?

2 George says, 'They broke into next door 7:30 one evening, lucky nobody was there, ransack the place, rape the maid.' What does this tell us about George?

3 George then tells with relish a story about a poor boy whose mother stumbled on Open Day, spilling the contents of the

basket she was carrying on her head. What else have you learnt about George from the story he has told?

✓ 4 Why does Len join with George in laughing at the story?

✓ 5 Why does Len laugh and laugh when George has gone?

✓ 6 Len speaks the last four words of Act One. What do they tell us about him?

Act Two

WK. 3/4
✓
Scene One

11 pages 41–3

After the intermission, the storytelling context is re-established: darkness, the light from striking a match, Pa Ben and his white rum, Pa Ben and his audience of actors on stage.

At the beginning of Act Two the play underlines some of the basic features of narrative. There is the hook of uncertainty. Following Len's laughter at the end of Act One, Pa Ben raises (through a Jamaican proverb) the possibility that Len may not laugh for long. Do we know Len's reasons for stalking George? What is the secret shared by George and Lois?

As at the beginning of Act One, we are reminded of the storyteller's freedom to invent material and to create suspense. 'Patience, everything in its time.'

Pa Ben says that Len told Lois that night about George McFarlane, but 'Him leave out a very important piece o' the story.' 'What him leave out?' 'Not just what, but why.'

✱
✓
Question

1 In what ways is the beginning of Act Two similar to the beginning of Act One?

86

12 pages 43–44

With Pa Ben present and actually telling the story, we see incidents acted out from Len's schooldays at Munro. The emphasis is on disparities of race and class reinforced by seniority in school. Then Pa Ben tells us that after school, Len, academically successful and black, can get no job at the bank other than manual labour; while light-skinned George, an academic failure, is given 'the keys to the vault'. Pa Ben outlines the development of George's fraudulent housing scheme

Note
page 46: both ends of the donkey – a stage donkey is sometimes created by two actors working together inside a donkey shape, one doing the front legs, the other the back. George is making a point about status.

✳ Question

✔ 1   George identifies three parts for Len in the Easter play. Why would George consider these roles suitable for Len? What do the choices tell us about George?

✔ **13 pages 44–8**

With Pa Ben commenting, phases of the housing racket are enacted. The scheme begins to fall apart, and George is under pressure.

Pa Ben tells us that Len has 'got the mongoose in a cage', but notes that '[w]hen you got a mongoose lock up, is then him dangerous'. George tells his business associate that Len is a 'definite possibility' and that George has the advantage of knowing Len's wife.

The action moves rapidly between Len's home and George, who is in panic. Len knows George's mode of operation and has set a trap for him. Len asks Lois whether she had run into George while working at Barclays Bank. Lois gives the impression she had not.

George telephones for the surname of Len's mother. Lois hangs up on him. George turns up in Pa Ben's district enquiring for Miss Aggy.

Questions

✓ 1 Outline the features of George's racket.

✓ 2 What goes wrong?

✓ 3 Why does George 'forage into people's bank accounts'?

✓ 4 George says, with reference to Len, 'Is a black man, I can handle him.' What does this tell us about George?

✓ 5 Why does George at first have difficulty locating Len's mother? What does this tell us about George and his assumptions? What does it tell us about Len?

✓ 6 'I'd say Mr Malcolm's got all the real estate he is likely to need.' Identify and explain the wit in Len's remark.

✓ 7 'McFarlane is vermin', says Len. 'I have a moral right to rid society of that sort of scum.' With your knowledge of the play as a whole, do you believe Len is motivated by moral righteousness, as is here implied? Why does he want to damage George?

✓ 8 While looking for Miss Aggy, George encounters Pa Ben. What does their brief encounter tell us about George and about Pa Ben?

Scene Two

✓ **14 pages 49–52**

Len is at home, going through the dossier on George, when Miss Aggy comes to visit. Miss Aggy reports that she has had a visit from George and that Pearl has died in childbirth. George has told Miss Aggy plausible lies and she is confident that all is well. She urges Len to help George out of his 'little financial difficulty'. She sees it as an opportunity to 'repay the debt' she and Len owe the family. Len tries to get Miss Aggy to consider some of the evidence, but she insists there is a debt of gratitude owed to George and Reverend Greaves, his father-in-law. Len angrily rejects the notion. He and Miss Aggy quarrel and nearly come to blows. She grabs him by the jacket; he picks up a chair. Miss Aggy seizes upon his action as evidence that he is not in control. She questions once again how he came to marry Lois. Miss Aggy moves like *a woman possessed with great religious fervour*. Holding Len *with great urgency* she declares: 'Your soul is in bondage! A have to release you! A have to set you

dossier – file containing information about a person, event, etc.

free!' She will counteract the obeah she believes has been put on Len.

Notes

page 51: 'If it was a damn drop o' water I had to give them to save they life, they woulda dead.' – Len's remark alludes to a passage from the Bible, Luke 16: 19–25, especially verse 24.

page 52: 'A have to set you free!' – Another passage from the Bible, John 8: 32.

Questions

1 Why does Miss Aggy say (again), 'Hold dog!'?

2 Why, on hearing Miss Aggy knock, does Len put on his shoes and his jacket and pick up his briefcase? What does this tell us about Len and his relationship with Miss Aggy?

3 Why does Len laugh when Miss Aggy tells him of George's visit to her, and his show of concern?

4 Why does Miss Aggy believe her money to be safe?

5 Why does Miss Aggy refuse to read the papers Len is urging her to read?

6 What does Miss Aggy say are her reasons for being convinced that Lois has set obeah on Len?

7 Miss Aggy says to Len, 'A have to set you free!' How does she propose to do this? Give evidence in support of your answer.

Scene Three

15 pages 53–6

Len visits Pa Ben, enquiring how to 'get some protection for Lois.' Pa Ben advises him to get Miss Aggy 'to stay her hand'. Len emphatically rejects Pa Ben's suggestion that he 'soften up' his mother and let George keep the money. Pa Ben insists that 'Obeah is a serious thing' and that if Len does not stop his mother, he may lose either Miss Aggy or Lois. Pa Ben wonders why Len is so obsessively determined to damage George. He recommends that Len 'join hands with Miss Lois' who 'may have a solution to the problem'. Len seems anxious to protect Lois but less concerned for the safety of his mother. Pa Ben gives the name and address of a lady named Mother Rachael.

Pa Ben runs into Miss Aggy who seems preoccupied and irritable. Sensing that she is on the verge of taking action, he sees a need to detain her the following day.

Note

page 54: high science – obeah

✳ Questions

✓ 1 Why does Len ask Pa Ben for water?

✓ 2 Pa Ben says, 'Praises be, the sun gone down. She can't do anything till tomorrow.' What does he think Miss Aggy intends to do?

✓ 3 Why is Len unwilling to go to a man in the district to seek 'protection for Lois'? What does this tell us about Len?

✓ 4 Pa Ben advises Len, 'You got to soften up your mother and give Mongoose the money.' Why does Len reject this suggestion so emphatically?

✓ 5 What does Pa Ben mean by 'the boomerang'?

✓ 6 What does he mean when he says to Len, 'You're a scientist, but you don't study high science yet'?

✓ 7 Pa Ben says to Len, 'Now tell me, what more important to you – mashin' up Mongoose life, or would you rather sacrifice one of the women you love?' At this point in the play, what do you think is most important to Len? Give evidence in support of your answer.

✓ 8 Pa Ben says to Len, 'Piece o' the story missin'. If not, your heart couldn't set so against him.' When are we given the missing piece? What is it?

✓ 9 What does Pa Ben mean when he says 'you have science and science'?

✓ 10 Pa Ben advises Len, 'join hands with Miss Lois. She may have the solution to the problem.' What is the solution? When does Len 'join hands' with Lois?

✓ 11 Why does Len say 'a hex'? What does his choice of language tell us about his education?

✓ 12 What does Pa Ben mean when he says 'Miss Lois is roots'?

✓ 13 How does the end of the play confirm that Pa Ben is right to suggest that 'love, trust and understanding' increase the chance of successfully fighting evil?

✓ 14 What reasons does Len give for being more concerned for Lois's safety than Miss Aggy's?

✓ 15 Why does Len ask Pa Ben to visit Mother Rachael for him? What does this tell us about Len?

✓ 16 What is Pa Ben trying to find out from Miss Aggy?

✓ 17 Why does he think he should detain her at home the next day?

Scene Four

✓ **16 pages 57–60**

Having consulted Mother Rachael, Len performs various rituals. The playwright advises that *'because ... Mother Rachael is a fraud ... her potions for protection and deliverance can be as farcical as possible.'* To telephone Mother Rachael for a clarification, Len disguises himself again, donning dark glasses, jacket and hat, and putting on an accent. The farce continues when Lois comes home. But under the frivolity there is an important point being made: Len is concerned for her safety. Lois finds his behaviour so uncharacteristic that she gets ready to receive bad news. Len continues his unusual display of affection. By the end of the scene, and to the bemusement of Lois, he is even signalling sexual eagerness.

Notes

page 60: Like Saul going to Damascus – see Acts 9.

page 60: The Virgin Mary – see Matthew 1: 18, Luke 1: 26–35, 2: 6–7.

Questions

✓ 1 What detail in her instructions does Mother Rachael clarify?

✓ 2 Lois says, 'Something terrible has happened.' Len replies, 'No, it won't.' What does Len's peculiar answer tell us about his state of mind?

✓ 3 Why does Lois say, 'Okay, now give me the bad news'?

✓ 4 Why does Lois say she thinks that the world has come to an end?

Scene Five

17 pages 61–2

Miss Aggy visits George at his home. George's wife is ill, having received a threat on George's life from a workman owed money. Miss Aggy reports that, but for Lois's influence, Len might already have given George help. Miss Aggy promises that in a day or two 'everything will come through' for George and Margaret.

✶ **Questions**

✔ 1 On hearing that a workman has threatened to kill him and that Margaret, his wife, is ill, Miss Aggy says to George, 'You don't deserve this.' What do you think? Give reasons for your answer.

✔ 2 Why does Miss Aggy believe 'Things goin' to be all right'?

Scene Six

18 pages 63–4

George pays Lois an angry visit. He accuses her of treachery, and says he will expose her if he has to. He rejects her overture of physical closeness. Len comes home, apparently happy. Though George confirms receipt of his message, George says he is 'reopening negotiations'. 'George has something to tell you', says Lois.

✶ **Questions**

✔ 1 Why is George angry with Lois?

✔ 2 Why does he think Miss Aggy's story is true?

19 pages 64–66

George's story is enacted. Bank Manager George has discovered that Lois has been illicitly borrowing from a client's account. Lois says she has had family-related financial difficulties while supporting a friend who is at university abroad. George declares a sexual interest in Lois and offers to sign the card which will put her out of danger. 'The choice is yours,' he says, 'for I can easily put this matter back on a strictly business basis.'

✔ 1 Why does George pick up the phone as though to call the police?

✔ 2 How did George persuade the customer there was nothing to worry about?

✔ 3 Why does George touch Lois? Why does he play with her blouse?

✔ 4 What does George mean when he says to Lois, 'On to brighter things, like how you planning to thank me'?

✔ 5 What does George mean when he says, 'I am a citizen above suspicion'? Is he 'above suspicion'?

✔ 6 What does George mean by 'a little relaxation'?

20 pages 66–7

Lois re-enters the present. She apologises to Len, who lovingly offers her immediate support: 'It's okay, sweetheart, we are in this together now.' George sneers at the show of affection. Lois, who says she has a headache, goes upstairs to lie down. George indicates his willingness to damage Len by spreading word of Lois's lapse and perhaps suggesting Len put her up to it. 'A man in your position can't afford a scandal.' Len grabs him by the collar. There is an urgent knocking at the door.

✗ **Question**

✔ 1 Why is the withdrawal slip signed by Lois 'no longer valid in a court of law'?

21 pages 67–70

Pa Ben enters, agitated. He tells Len that Mother Rachael is a fraud. On hearing that Lois has a headache, Pa Ben fears the worst, and again advises Len to negotiate with Miss Aggy. Then he indicates George as the 'only hope', thinking no doubt – as he later implies (page 74) – that Len will make peace with George in the presence of Miss Aggy. Len asks Pa Ben to find Miss Aggy and bring her back. Pa Ben urges Len to tell Lois everything.

Len hands George a dossier to read. 'After all,' says Len, 'it's your life story.'

Pa Ben sets out. His mission is conducted at the same time as George's perusal of the dossier. Words from one strand of the narrative occasionally connect meaningfully with words from the other.

Frightened by the dossier, George offers to get and to relinquish the original document. But Len turns the screws. He summarises incriminating evidence of illegal acts by George. He threatens prison for George and family. George is made to grovel. Len requires George to tell all when Miss Aggy arrives. 'Not just about the house …' 'What else is there?' asks George, and Len replies: 'Among other things, Cassava Nova. … At Munro, by the old bell tower. … Leave nothing out.'

There is a knocking at the door. After their country bus journey, Pa Ben and Miss Aggy have arrived.

✳ Questions

✔ 1 Finding Len in conversation with George, Pa Ben apologises for interrupting. He says, 'Cry excuse, beg pardon, forgive mi manners.' He last exchanged words with George on pages ~~47–4~~ 8 What does Pa Ben's conduct in the two encounters tell us about him?

✔ 2 When he is told that Lois has a headache, Pa Ben says 'Oh my God!' Why is he so concerned?

✔ 3 Why might an audience laugh when Pa Ben says 'But I been telling you that all the time'? What does Pa Ben really mean?

✔ 4 Why might an audience laugh again when Pa Ben says 'More or less'? Is he at this point mainly a storyteller or a character in the story? Give reasons for your answer.

✔ 5 When showing George photostats of incriminating withdrawal slips signed by George, Len points out that they are '[a]ll within the last seven years, [and] therefore valid in law'. With what is he contrasting these slips?

✔ 6 When George asks Len, 'What do you want me to do, clean your shoes?' the situation enacted on page 46 has been reversed. What should we understand from the comparison?

Pa Ben comments. He had brought Miss Aggy back, thinking Len might 'settle up with Mongoose in front of her' but instead Len started 'to replay the story of his youth in the days when Mama drumbeat Miss Margaret so much in him head. Miss Margaret; Advancement; Advancement; till him gone like a fool write love-letter to the girl'.

The Cassava Nova incident is enacted. Margaret has been offended by Len's grandiloquent love-letter, and says her father would have a heart attack if he saw it. George tells her to reply to the letter from Len, inviting him to meet her after lights-out. George and the other boys will be waiting for him.

'In the darkness Len screams, terrible and long. A spotlight picks him up as he appears in the auditorium.' He has been sexually humiliated. He is taunted by George: 'Next time we cut it off. ... You cassava-nova you.'

Len's entry through the auditorium, like Pa Ben's at the beginning of the play, encourages the audience to identify closely with him. This is the enactment, for which we have been made to wait, of a major reason for Len's consuming malice towards George. This is the 'very important piece o' the story', the missing 'why' to which Pa Ben referred at the beginning of Act Two (page 45).

Miss Aggy moves to assault the 'wicked evil wretch', but George escapes.

Notes

page 70: the perpendicular meet the contuberance, which in lay the conbrucksion' – the words sound imposing, but their meaning is uncertain. 'Perpendicular' suggests the beginning of a metaphor from geometry, but 'contuberance' and 'conbrucksion' appear to be inventions. The Jamaican tea-meeting, and various other traditions of the 'man of words' in the Caribbean, thrive on creative grandiloquence.

page 72: cassava-nova – a coinage which writes the tuber (cassava, connoting rural, peasant) into a version of Casanova, a name for a womaniser, skilled in the art of seduction. Giacomo Casanova de Seingalt (1725–98) was an Italian adventurer.

Questions

1 Why does Len write Margaret a 'love-letter'?

2 Why does Margaret take offence?

3 What does the passage quoted from the letter tell us about the education of Len?

4 Margaret says, of Reverend Greaves, 'God knows, he's a generous man, but he expects those people to know their place.' What does she mean by 'those people'? What does the statement tell us about Margaret?

5 Margaret describes Miss Aggy as 'a rather ignorant unfortunate dragon of a mother … always bowing and scraping, wheedling her way into father's favour.' In Act One (page 34) Miss Aggy sends greetings by George to Miss Margaret, 'from an old friend'. What does this disparity tell us about the relationship between Miss Aggy and the Greaves family?

6 What purpose is accomplished by Margaret's reply to Len?

7 What have George and the other boys done to Len?

8 George tells Len, 'Don't forget.' Does Len forget?

9 Why does Miss Aggy try to attack George?

10 Why, in your opinion, does the playwright let George escape?

---

23 pages 72–4

The final movement. Miss Aggy, acknowledging her error, seeks to atone for her sins. From here until the end, the language of the play is more insistently religious than before. Len tells Miss Aggy that after his Cassava Nova trauma he ran away from school and stayed away for a week, cared for by a 'good Samaritan and his daughter'. When Miss Aggy expresses a wish to thank them, they are revealed to be Lois and Lois's father, now deceased. Len reaffirms his love for Lois, then for Miss Aggy. Expecting the boomerang of forces she has set in motion, Miss Aggy is saying goodbyes. She does not want night to catch her on the road.

Lois, barring the door, begins reciting the twenty-third psalm. Pa Ben and Len join in and, holding hands, the three of them encircle Miss Aggy as she tries to escape. They break into a chant, a *'prayer for her deliverance from the evil spirits.'* Their united effort finally defeats the power of the boomerang. They knew, as Pa Ben declares, 'that the one force that could counteract all evil was there, and that force was love.'

For Pa Ben, as for many audiences, the sight of Miss Aggy, Len and Lois, a family together at last, is deeply moving. *'He starts to cry in his joyfulness.'* He says, 'All well' and the lights go down.

Notes

page 73: A Good Samaritan – See Luke 10: 30–7.

page 73: I am a foolish old woman – cf. Shakespeare, *King Lear IV* vii 60: 'I am a very foolish fond old man.'

page 74: Omia n Twi. Mia Kuru. Omia n ani. – The chant is intended to suggest an African language. (See the section on Obeah.)

Questions

1 Len says, of Lois, 'I love her.' He says to Miss Aggy, 'I love you.' Has he said so earlier in the play? Why is he saying so now?

2 Stage directions near the end ask for 'silence as the circle is bathed in a warm rich light'. Why?

3 Miss Aggy says, 'My children, my children.' What is the main significance of these, her final, words?

Chronologically speaking

As we have seen, the story is not told in chronological order. If told in chronological order, the story might go something like this:

Miss Aggy, a marketwoman who contends that 'anything black nuh good', is determined that her son, Len Tomlinson, shall escape the restrictions of black poverty. She pushes him to break free through education and through marriage to a light-skinned wife, drumming into his head that the person for him is Margaret, daughter of the Reverend Greaves. Miss Aggy's good friend, Pa Ben, does not agree with her attitude to blackness or with her programme for Len.

Len wins a scholarship to an elitist school, Munro. He is humiliated there by light-skinned boys who despise him for being black and regard his poverty as laughable. Obsessed with the ambition taught him by his mother, Len writes a sort of love-letter to Margaret Greaves. Alarmed and offended to think that a black boy of low status might think her accessible, she shares the letter with her light-skinned friend George. As instructed by George she replies to Len, inviting him to meet her. When he arrives, Len is set upon by McFarlane and some other boys who subject him to sexual humiliation, with threats of even greater violence.

Len runs away from school, but is accommodated for a week by a kind black family who have a daughter named Lois. Len and Lois become friends. Len goes away on a scholarship to study economics in England, and Lois helps to support him. But when her father dies and there are other unexpected family expenses Lois, who is working in a bank, starts 'borrowing' from accounts. Her illegal activity is discovered by her Bank Manager, George McFarlane, who blackmails her into having sex with him.

At first, Len rarely writes to his mother from England. Miss Aggy wonders whether someone in the village has set obeah on him. At the urging of Pa Ben, with whom he has been in touch through Lois, Len begins to write more often. One of his letters informs Miss Aggy that he has married Lois and he encloses a picture of the couple. Miss Aggy, distressed that he has married black, is convinced that Lois has set obeah on Len. Miss Aggy quarrels with Pa Ben, who has criticised her attitude. It is a year before she accepts his friendship again.

Len returns home with his wife and a doctorate. Miss Aggy tells of having made a down payment on a house, on the recommendation of George McFarlane. Len investigates the scheme and finds evidence that it is crooked.

Miss Aggy, visiting Len in Kingston, is hostile to Lois, who retaliates. George McFarlane, who has come to see Len Tomlinson at home, is surprised to learn that Lois is Mrs Tomlinson. She asks him not to reveal that they have ever known each other. When Len arrives, George, in desperate need of financial support, shows himself to be very nervous, mentions that he is married to Margaret, and reveals his suspicion that an enemy has been trying to destroy him. Len assesses George's business proposition and gives a discouraging answer. George raises the possibility of a personal deal with Len, who says he will consider it. The two reminisce about Munro, but George seems not to remember Len. Encouraged by drink and Len's apparent good humour, George tells an anecdote about a poor boy and his mother. Len reveals that he was the boy in the story. George leaves in a hurry, embarrassed. After George's departure Len expresses the animosity he had concealed.

Miss Aggy asks Len to help George financially, insisting that she and Len owe a debt of gratitude to George's in-laws, the Greaves family. Len angrily disputes the debt. He and Miss Aggy quarrel and he seizes a chair, as if to hit her with it. The incident persuades Miss Aggy that some evil force controls her son. She says she has to set him free.

Len asks Pa Ben for advice on how to get protection for Lois. After some hesitation, Pa Ben tells him of a Mother Rachael. Len goes to her, and performs the rituals she instructs.

Miss Aggy tells George that, but for the influence of Lois, Len might have given him the help he needs. Believing himself betrayed by Lois, George decides to use what he knows about her as a lever against Len. But when George tells the story of her misconduct Len is lovingly supportive of Lois. Pa Ben comes to report that Mother Rachael is a bogus obeah woman and that protection offered by her rituals must therefore be ineffectual. Urging Len to make peace with George in the presence of Miss Aggy, Pa Ben goes to fetch her. Len gives George a dossier to read, with evidence of illegalities by George.

When Pa Ben returns with Miss Aggy, Len orders George to tell Miss Aggy the story of his cruelty to Len after Len's letter to Margaret. Miss Aggy moves to attack George, who escapes. Miss Aggy, recognising her errors at last, begs forgiveness and prepares to leave, expecting that the evil she has wrongfully set in motion against Lois will boomerang on her. But Lois, ready to take risks for Miss Aggy, starts a ritual to undo the evil. Len and Pa Ben join in, and Miss Aggy is saved. She acknowledges Lois and Len as her children.

Questions

1 Why is the information in the play not given in this order?
2 In the chronological summary, find two pieces of information which the playwright withholds for a while.
3 What does the playwright gain by withholding the information?
4 In his note on Costumes the playwright suggests 'a simple device to help the flashbacks'. Find a flashback and act it out in class, paying close attention to the stage directions. Why does the playwright suggest these choices? Discuss other ways in which the flashbacks might be presented on stage.

People, Values And Social Context

✔

Old Story Time talks about Jamaica in the three or four decades before 1980 (page 55).

The play notes changes in the status of black people. In the earlier part, Miss Aggy says to her son, 'life is hard when you black, but with a little education you still have a chance' (page 11). Academically successful at a prestigious high school, he is nevertheless too black for a job in the bank, where fair-skinned employees are still the norm (pages 12, 43).[1] While he is studying in England, the policy has begun to change: the bank has hired his girl-friend, who is black (page 66). In the 1970s, however, when socialism is in vogue (page 38), black Len, newly returned from England with a doctorate in economics, wields power in the Development Bank (page 35).

While Len graduates into the urban middle-class, Miss Aggy stubbornly remains peasant. Unlike Len and Lois, whose home impresses George (page 33), Miss Aggy lives in a wattle-and-daub house (page viii) where pigs may be sleeping under the bed (page 32). She will not agree to have a gas stove or a water closet. She fears that neighbours might be envious. 'Next thing people malice me off, then come lick me down say me live in big house' (page 24). She does not wish to change her living conditions.

The picture *Old Story Time* presents of recent decades reflects the longer historical legacy. In the interaction between African black people and British whites on sugar plantations, power and status resided with whiteness. Many black people (but, of course, not all) internalised a notion of white superiority, and transmitted self-contempt from generation to generation.

Miss Aggy is part of that line. Not only does she believe that 'anything black nuh good' (page 18); she tries to teach her son that this is so. If her attitude is 'ignorance', as it is deemed by both Pa Ben and Len (pages 20, 55), it is useful to ask (as Pa Ben does), 'Born and bred of what?' (page 55). Conditioned by history and her social experience, she accepts the 'white bias' of her society.[2] She considers that, for Len, advancement is 'a nice brown girl with tall hair down to her back.' She insists that he avoid 'the little dutty black gal dem in the district' (page 11), but in fact she will object to any black woman claiming his attention. She is distressed to learn that Len has married someone black – 'Me nuh want her beside mi son' (page 19). She thinks Lois must have won him by obeah. She remains hostile to her daughter-in-law – 'Tar baby' (page 28), 'Black Sambo' (page 52) – until very near the end of the play when the truth is revealed.

Miss Aggy believes 'You should know yuh place' (page 51). Uncritically subservient to fair-skinned people, she is completely taken in by George McFarlane. 'I know you wouldn't give me bad advice,' she says. 'Is God send you here to guide and look after me' (page 31). She is inordinately grateful. She credits Reverend Greaves with having helped make Len the man he is. (Which is true, ironically: Reverend Greaves and family have helped make Len the bitter man he is. He wants his mother to 'stop bow down an' worship them people like them was God.') 'Where is yuh gratitude?' Miss Aggy wants to know (page 51). She sends greetings to George's wife, Margaret, 'from an old friend' (page 30), but Margaret used to regard her as a pest, 'always bowing and scraping' (page 71) to impress Reverend Greaves.

Miss Aggy's true friend, Pa Ben, does not share all her attitudes to race. Though he associates Africa with savages and cannibals, and England with deliverance (page 19), he is not, like her, preoccupied with colour. 'What's so wrong,' he asks, 'if the boy just want to marry somebody who look like him own mother, eh?' (page 20). Pa Ben is not overawed by fair-skinned people. He is surprised 'to see a big white man in these parts an' is nuh election time', and his 'spirit never take to' George (page 47). He finds George lacking in courtesy.

As represented by George McFarlane and Margaret Greaves, the fair-skinned people are contemptuous of blacks. At Munro[3] they are, according to Pa Ben, 'sneering down on the world, them head way up in the sky, drunk with power and authority' (page 42). 'Clean my shoes,' George orders Len, 'burnish it till you see your big black ugly face in it, boy!' (page 42).

The pattern continues after schooldays. The fair-skinned people consider themselves superior.[4] Len, an academic success, cannot get employment in the bank, 'only manual labour' (page 43), but George – 'duncey Mongoose who never pass one subject' – is offered a job (page 43). When George, promoted to bank manager, has to deal with Lois, 'one of the first black girls that the bank employ', he threatens, 'Think, what it would do for your race if the

courteous – polite, considerate
contempt – feeling that a person or thing deserves scorn or extreme reproach

news was to get out …'. George clearly sees himself as very much separate from black people. Yet, like many plantation whites in Jamaican history, he is not averse to having sex with black women. Leering, he tells Lois: 'as a man I couldn't sit back and see an attractive girl like you go to waste in some dirty prison, just for a few dollars' (page 66).

Even when George approaches Len for help, he still assumes himself superior. 'Is a black man, I can handle him', he tells his business associate (page 46). George disapproves of changes at Munro. 'Packed now with a bunch o' riff-raff, scholarship-winners. Sacred walls, man, desecrated' (page 38). Casually contemptuous, he reports on a crime: 'They broke into next door 7:30 one evening, lucky nobody was there, ransack the place, rape the maid' (page 38). As George perceives the world, the maid is nobody.

Attitudes to power and authority

Miss Aggy's attitude to power and authority is inseparable from her attitude to light-skinned people. In her experience, those are the people in charge. She is subservient to them and inordinately grateful for any assistance they may offer. So she is flattered by George's attention in the bank. 'I was surprised, couldn't figure out what this high posh white gentleman wanted with the likes o' poor little me' (page 32). Unlike Pa Ben who demands respect and courtesy even from 'a big white man' (page 47), Miss Aggy accepts – indeed, insists on – her low status. She thinks Len should be grateful to the Greaves family, even for what he calls 'the two scraps from their table' (page 51). Len is resentful: 'When they eat and leave they throw it to me in the kitchen, like I was a damn stray.' Miss Aggy finds Len's attitude outrageous. 'You did want to eat with them 'round the table? You did give dem anyt'ing to put down? They didn't have to give you anything, you know' (page 51).

Their son-in-law, George McFarlane, revels in power and authority, which he abuses. The bully at school (pages 42–3, 71–2), 'drunk with power and authority' (page 42), becomes the bank manager, 'a citizen above suspicion' (page 66), who takes advantage of Lois. He assumes that people of his colour should be in control. He says of Len, 'Is a black man, I can handle him' (page 46).

He is wrong this time. When Len acquires power, he focuses on getting back at George. He pursues him relentlessly, 'chasing the bugger for months' (page 46). He toys with him, patronises him, plays status games that show George who is boss. 'My secretary gave you a message, didn't she?' (page 63). George is at his mercy in the end. 'Jesus Christ, man, if you want me to beg, I will beg. ... I'll do anything' (page 69).

Dreams and aspirations

Miss Aggy has dreams and aspirations for Len. When he is still a boy, she tells him: 'life is hard when you black, but with a little education you still have a chance. When time come for you to have girlfriend, A have a nice girl pick out for you. Miss Margaret, Reverend Greaves' daughter, a nice brown girl with tall hair down to her back. She is advancement, you hear me.' (page 11)

When Len seems well on the road to advancement through education, Miss Aggy regards her project as incomplete: Len should marry Miss Margaret, 'Is mi dream,' Miss Aggy declares (page 15).

That dream causes problems for Len. The idea has been drummed into his head. 'Miss Margaret: Advancement; Advancement; till him gone like a fool write love-letter to the girl' (page 70). When Margaret is offended by Len's letter, George and some other boys decide to teach him a lesson. After the traumatic experience, Len remains bitter for years.

Family relationships

Although – or perhaps because – Miss Aggy loves her son, she gives him little freedom as a boy. Even when Len is an adult, she tries to tell him what to do. She objects to Lois, is discourteous to her, and eventually tries to do her serious harm. But Miss Aggy, though she makes bad mistakes, believes that she is acting in the interests of her son. She 'only wanted what was best for him' (page 20).

Len cares about his mother, but less than she cares about him. Begged to do so by Pa Ben, he writes to her from England more

frequently than at first (page 18). He brings Miss Aggy a present from England, and seems concerned about her cough (page 23).
He has sent her money to improve her living conditions and he argues that she deserves to be more comfortable (page 24). But, especially as she is so relentlessly hostile to Lois, Len finds his mother tiresome. Hearing her at the gate can tempt him to pretend he is going out (page 49). He says her attitude to Lois is 'ignorance'. When he begins to fear for Lois's safety, he becomes (for a time) indifferent to his mother's possible fate. 'At this point I just don't care' (page 55).

Though Lois has described him as 'not given to affection' (page 27), Len shows his love when he thinks she is in danger: and, when he has been told of her troubles at the bank and with George, he is lovingly supportive. 'It's okay, sweetheart, we are in this together now' (page 66).

After George, as instructed, has told Miss Aggy of Len's traumatic experience at Munro, Len declares his love for his mother as well as Lois. His mother, at risk from the 'boomerang', is rescued by a ritual led by Lois. Generously forgiven, and saved from the consequences of her misjudgement, Miss Aggy gratefully acknowledges her son and daughter-in-law: 'My children, my children.' Pa Ben is overjoyed to see 'the three of them together as a family' (page 74).

Women in society ✔

In an obvious sense, Pearl is a minor character: she makes few appearances, has few lines, and is reported dead long before the play has come to an end. Yet she is important to the overall meaning of the work, and in many productions is theatrically memorable.

She first appears as a child in the village playing with Len. The scene suggests Len's longing for a normal childhood and Miss Aggy's pressure on him to be different. Pearl accuses him of 'turning into a real high posh' (page 10) under pressure from his mother. The scene also makes vivid the village temptations to early sexual activity. 'Go on like you is a big man.' 'Big man, yes.' 'In yuh pants.' 'You want to see it?' (page 10). 'A don't want yuh mother to beat you, you know. [As she pushes herself even closer to him.]' (page 10). We are soon told she is repeatedly pregnant: 'So the ol' careless boy them lash her, is so she breed.'

At twenty she already has five children. 'She mash up bad' (page 14).

Her name is ironic: she seems a pearl of no price;[5] and Pearl is the brand name of a contraceptive pill. She is a measure of what Miss Aggy, with all her faults, has managed to save Len from. Miss Aggy tells Pa Ben, 'When me look on her, an' think say if me never did fight an' struggle with the one Mass Len, all now him would be knocking 'bout the district a turn wutliss like the rest a them' (page 18). As indicated in the note on Costumes, her appearances suggest the passage of time. Each time she appears, she has more children and looks more broken down. When Len returns from England, immaculately suited, somewhat formal and a little cold, the gap between them is unforgettable.

'Here you are, for the baby when it comes.' (page 22)

Having the actress who plays Pearl play Margaret also – which Rhone recommends – may be not just a matter of convenience, like having her play the real estate developer; it may also be part of the play's symbolic pattern. There is a contrast between Pearl and Len who, from similar starting-places, travel divergent routes; and there is a contrast also between two women – one light-skinned and one black – dealt very different hands by circumstances in a white-biased society. That the name Margaret means 'a pearl' reinforces the symbolic point.

Pearl slops around the village, having babies, until her early death (page 49). Miss Aggy has different standards. She pointedly removes Pa Ben's hand when it rests on her thigh (page 14). She has one son, whose father is not mentioned in the play. She is ambitious for Len, pushing him, and making sacrifices for him (page 24). Miss Aggy fits the stereotype of the strong black woman living for her family – like Mama Younger in *A Raisin in the Sun*[6] or Sophia in *Moon on Rainbow Shawl*.[7] But she seems to assume that women exist to serve men. When the adult Len offers her a drink, her remark – 'So you is the manservant' (page 28) – implies that he is doing Lois's work.

Lois has a different perspective. She protests that she is being neglected by Len. She makes the point several times in her first scene (page 26). Miss Aggy aggravates the tension between Lois and Len, communicating disapproval of Lois in many ways, including hints that Lois does not feed Len properly and does not keep the house clean (page 26). But the audience get to know that Lois has – like Miss Aggy – made sacrifices for Len and for her family. Although she is not a mother, she has carried the responsibility of a single parent. She explains to George: 'my father died, and me being the eldest, all the responsibility for the younger ones fell on me.' In spite of the burden, she continued supporting Len when he was studying in England (page 63), eventually putting herself at risk to keep on sending him money.

In return for not calling in the police, George exploits her sexually. Like Pearl, though in different circumstances and with no visible consequences, she is a woman victimised. Len does not learn until later how much she has endured for him.

Lois is most important, however, not as a wife or mistress or substitute mother but as a paragon of Christian forgiveness. She readily forgives Miss Aggy who, until a minute or two before, had shown her nothing but hostility.

Obeah

The word obeah is 'used in Jamaica to denote witchcraft, evil magic or sorcery by which supernatural power is invoked to achieve personal protection or the destruction of enemies.'

Miss Aggy and Pa Ben take the existence of obeah for granted. When she has not had a letter from Len, she wonders whether 'somebody in the district burn a candle on his head'. 'Who in the district,' asks Pa Ben, incredulous, 'would do a thing like that?' Miss Aggy has plenty of candidates: 'in they heart they malice me off, jealous say mi son doing too well.' (page 13)

When a letter Miss Aggy receives from Len seems much too short and formal, her suspicions deepen: 'Somebody or something turning mi son against me. ... Evil forces at work' (page 18). When Len sends a photograph of him and Lois, the black woman he has married, Miss Aggy thinks again that obeah must be involved (page 19). Realising what she might do, Pa Ben warns: 'before you ... go set evil forces at work to try an' hit back at the chile, consider the one chance you might be wrong, an' when you done consider that, consider the consequences' (page 20).

Miss Aggy does not act immediately. Only after her son has seemed about to strike her with a chair does she feel certain enough: 'after your performance here today, raise yuh hand to kill yuh Ma, there is no power on God's earth could convince me say is not obeah that woman obeah you' (page 52).

If Miss Aggy gets something set on Lois, and Lois has effective protection against it, Miss Aggy is left 'wide open for the boomerang' (page 53). Pa Ben expresses this concern to Len who does not understand, and at this juncture does not really care. 'Mama took her chance, she knew the consequences' (page 55).

When Mother Rachael turns out to be 'an impostor, a bogus' (page 67), Pa Ben is agitated because this means that Lois does not have the protection Len thought he had arranged by following Mother Rachael's instructions. As a stage direction indicates, *'we will later discover that Mother Rachael is a fraud, so her potions for protection and deliverance can be as farcical as possible'* (page 58). The mumbo-jumbo in Act Two Scene Four does not make fun of obeah itself. The play, through Pa Ben, tells us: 'Obeah is a serious thing. Don't meddle with it' (page 54).

At the end, when Miss Aggy learns she owes a debt of gratitude to Lois, whom she had taken to be evil, she fears that the forces she directed against Lois will boomerang on her. 'Help me, oh Lord! Give me the strength to do what I have to do before the sun go down!' (page 73).

Lois knows what to do, and the risks involved. She leads a ritual to counteract the evil and to save her mother-in-law. The ritual begins with the twenty-third psalm. In the chant that follows, Rhone has borrowed African words from a passage in Leonard Barrett's *The Sun and the Drum*:

> The possession crisis in *Kumina* is known as *myal*, that stage of *Kumina* when the spirit of an ancestor actually takes control of the dancer's body, at which time the dancer loses control of speech and faculties and is actually the ancestor. The origin of the word *myal* is very difficult to trace. The only word that comes near in Twi is the word *mia*, which means 'to press' or 'to squeeze'. It is a word which, when combined with other words, lends itself to the behaviour patterns of one who is possessed. For example, *mia kuru* means 'to dress or treat a wound or sore with water or medicine'. *Omia n ani means* 'he shuts his eyes, he meditates, he exerts himself'.[9]

In many productions the snatches of Twi seem powerful and strange. They invoke ancestral Africa and, in tandem with the twenty-third psalm, enable spiritual healing. Myal is 'An old religion concerned with healing in Jamaica ... [W]hat has remained at the core of Myal has been the inseparable link between healing and religion. Belief in such a linkage was brought from Africa.'[10]

Jamaican folk culture

The play reflects Jamaican culture. Christianity is a pervasive cultural reference, and obeah is taken to be a fact of life. As Pa Ben puts it: 'you have science and science' (page 55): science as in mathematics and chemistry, science as in obeah. There are problems computers cannot solve. The dead require respect and may assist the living. Pa Ben warns Miss Aggy against seeming to slight the ghost of Pa Zaccy, a peevish postman (page 16), credits Pa Zaccy's ghost with having caused a letter to arrive from Len (page 17), and sprinkles a little rum on the ground as a mark of gratitude.

When the storyteller says 'What sweet nanny goat …', his audience completes the Jamaican proverb (page 41). Children's games, folksongs, hymns and parodies of hymns help to sustain the ambience of Jamaican folk culture. 'The bull frog jump from bank to bank' (page 8) and 'Change the house round' (page 25) are reminiscent of children's games. 'Rock of ages' (page 9) is a very popular hymn in rural Jamaica. 'Rice an' peas / An' coconut oil' (page 16) is a parody sometimes sung at nine-night ceremonies (to the tune of hymn 314 in *Hymns Ancient and Modern*, 'As pants the hart for cooling streams'). In the nine-night ceremony – 'to give the deceased person a good departure from this world' – there is often humour[11] and jollification. 'Sly Mongoose' is a well-known Jamaican folksong, appropriately applied to the evasive rascal, George.

Rumour and gossip

The play suggests that in Jamaica rumour and gossip are factors to be reckoned with. In the village, Miss Aggy would hate to have her neighbours know that Len has not been writing her from England. 'Me nuh want them to spread it around the district say him dash me 'way. Me just have to keep up the pretence' (page 14). So she lies to Pearl. We learn much about Pearl from gossipy exchanges between Miss Aggy and Pa Ben (pages 14–15). When Miss Aggy and Pa Ben realise that Pearl has overheard the reading of Len's brief letter and seen Miss Aggy's disappointment, they hurry after her 'to buy her silence' (page 18). Pa Ben, narrating, remarks that 'If that news did get out, it would spread like bush fire' (page 18). Furthermore, if people learnt that Pa Ben was in touch with Len, they might say that he set obeah on Len (page 18).

Rumour is similarly a force in middle-class life. When Len writes to Margaret at school, George warns of the possibility of 'rumour … with all the nasty innuendoes' (page 71). In the business world years later, George talks of 'an orchestrated plan' to ruin him, spreading '[m]alicious, insidious lies' (page 35). Len seems to have heard, and perhaps fostered, some of them. Miss Aggy has heard some rumours about George but, in her mistaken loyalty, refuses to consider evidence they may be true (pages 50–4). George points out to Len that, although the withdrawal slip incriminating Lois is no longer valid in a court of law, it can be used to damage Len. 'A man in your position can't afford a scandal. This is a small town, word travels fast. plus you never know how I will twist the story when I release it' (page 67). No wonder Len, in search of protection for Lois, declines to visit a man in Pa Ben's village – 'too close to home' (page 53) – and disguises himself and his voice to visit Mother Rachael (page 57). He is afraid of gossip.

Christianity and the Bible

The play is full of references to God, Christ and the Bible, some centrally important, many helping to sustain the play's religious tone. Though only in a metaphor, Pa Ben in the very first moments mentions church – 'you people mouth join church or what?' (page 6). Soon he reports the promise of politicians 'to bring down the moon, cut it up and hang it 'pon stick so we could read bible when night come' (page 7). Returning from the market, Miss Aggy has brought Pa Ben a hymn book, and when he sings a snatch of 'Rock of Ages' she pounces: 'So you going to service tomorrow?' Pa Ben is not too sure, and Miss Aggy knows he is avoiding the commitment. 'Old devil' she calls him, affectionately (page 9).

Far from being a devil, he is a virtual saint, a model of Christian virtue. But he does not constantly quote the Bible or call on the name of God; Miss Aggy has more of that tendency. She says such things as 'Lawd a mercy!' (page 13), 'Holy fathers in heaven! Thank you, Jesus! You answer mi prayer' (page 17), 'Give God thanks' (pages 22, 27), 'These are the last days. Praise God I won't be here much longer' (page 29), 'Is God send you here to guide and look after me, you know' (page 31). 'Jesus, Saviour, hold mi hand!'. 'Take this cross, Saviour!', 'Oh Lord, forgive him!' (pages 50-51). But she is often undermined by what her religious references imply. 'Jesus Saviour, pilot me,' she says, about to punish Len. 'If you run A murder you tonight' (page 10). (If piloted by Jesus, would she be so severe?) At the end of Act Two Scene Two, when Len picks up a chair as if about to hit Miss Aggy with it, he comes to his senses and says, 'I'm sorry, Mama.' But she, in spite of the religious language she employs, dismisses his contrition. She is not about to forgive him (as Lois will forgive her at the end). 'Sorry?' she says. 'Sorry can't help situation. You always sorry (page 52).' She cannot forgive his trespasses. She begins to list them instead, flying in the face of the Lord's Prayer.[12] And when, soon after, she cries out to Len, 'Your soul is in bondage! … A have to set you free!' (page 52) she is echoing John 8: 32: 'And ye shall know the truth, and the truth shall make you free.' She does not know the truth; she is in fact mistaken, and will put herself in jeopardy.

When Len, in quarrelling with Miss Aggy, says 'Jesus Christ' (pages 51, 52) the expression is a profanity, as from George (pages 34, 37, 45, 69). George also introduces a religious reference with a social sneer: the parts he would assign to Len in the Easter play are 'Judas Iscariot, one of the thieves, and both ends of the donkey'. Pa Ben, narrating, continues the Palm Sunday allusion: 'They beat him black behind till it turn blue, all o' them playing Jesus, and they ride him into Jerusalem!' (page 43). In the Mother Rachael scene (Act Two Scene Four), there is religious allusion also, heavily ironic, prefiguring the final moments of the play. Len will indeed be suddenly converted, like Saul on the road to Damascus; and, like the Immaculate Conception (page 60), Len's re-entry into love will be a redemptive miracle. The extended pattern of religious reference culminates in the closing moments of the play. The language there is most insistently religious. 'Lawd, mi spirit in bondage. I have to atone for mi sins. I have to cleanse mi soul. … [F]orgive me, please, forgive me.' 'A good Samaritan and his daughter took care of me …' 'Heaven rest his soul!', 'The Lord is my shepherd.' 'All night long we pray. We pray for strength in this the vigil of the long night.' (pages 72–4).

Love

At the end of the play, with great emotion, Pa Ben speaks of love as 'the one force that could counteract all evil' (page 74). *Old Story Time* is a play in praise of love.

In her domineering manner, Miss Aggy loves her son. 'A only want what is best for you,' she says, but 'Mama knows best' (page 11). To have her judgement questioned is bewildering. 'I only wanted what was best for him' (page 20). She has made sacrifices for Len (page 24), and when she fears she is about to die, is still thinking of his welfare. 'Just take care of mi son, is all I ask' (page 73). But she has pushed him into situations which have caused him pain, and some of his most unhappy memories are associated with the values she advanced. When she is made vividly aware of some of what he has suffered, and acknowledges how mistaken she has been, Len can say at last, 'I love you, Mama' (page 73).

Pa Ben throughout is a model of love in action. He cares deeply about his friend, Miss Aggy, but would temper her severity with Len (page 19). He knows that, though he disagrees with some of her values, her primary concern is for her son. 'Black was good enough for me. It not good enough for him' (page 20). Recognising her colour prejudice as an obstacle to love, Pa Ben tries to lead her away from 'ignorance' (page 20). When she is ordering him off her property, he is still giving her good advice: 'consider the one chance that you might be wrong, an' when you done consider that, consider the consequences.' She withholds her speech from him, but Pa Ben does not give up. His habitual behaviour fits the definition by St Paul in I Corinthians 13: 4–7:

> Love is patient and kind; it is not jealous or conceited or proud; love is not ill-mannered or selfish or irritable; love does not keep a record of wrongs; love is not happy with evil, but is happy with the truth. Love never gives up; and its faith, hope and patience never fail.[13]

'It hurt mi soul case how she was going on', says Pa Ben. 'After all, she was mi best friend. A had to keep trying, for me is not one to keep up malice' (page 21).

Malice is the enemy of love. Pa Ben is good at sensing malice, and he tries to root it out. Although Miss Aggy kept up 'One piece a malice' (pages 20-21) against him, his patience wins her over. But only, apparently, where he himself is concerned. He knows that 'in her heart of hearts' she is still 'carrying feelings' for Lois (page 21). He prevails upon her to the extent that she stays her hand, allowing for the chance she may be wrong. When eventually she thinks that she is certain, she complains of having 'against [her] better judgement' kept the peace (page 52). Pa Ben, on the other hand, is committed to peace and love. When, earlier, he discerns that Len is 'carrying feelings' for his mother, having failed to write her a proper letter from England, Pa Ben tries to comfort her (page 16), and urges Len 'to make the peace' (page 18), which gradually he does. Pa Ben sees that Pearl is 'carrying feelings' against Miss Aggy' (page 18) and he counsels her not to spread the news of Len's neglect. And later, detecting the malice which has made Len blind to more important matters, he recommends that Len 'soften up [his] mother and give Mongoose the money' (page 53). But Len does not desire peace. Pa Ben puts to him the crucial question: 'what more important to you – mashin' up Mongoose life, or would you rather sacrifice one of the women you love?' (page 54).

It is important to recognise that, although it gives us reasons why Len is harbouring malice (against his mother, the Greaves family and George McFarlane), the play is critical of that malice. Len's remembered hurts distract him from the duty and the rewards of love. He can profess not to care what happens to his mother, dismissing the danger to her as strictly her responsibility: 'Mama took her chance, she knew the consequences' (page 55). Len's resentments affect all his relationships, including his relationship with Lois. For most of the play – until he fears that Lois's life is threatened – he is, as she complains, 'not given to affection' (page 27). Because he has resentful memories of the Greaves family – 'When they eat and leave they throw it to me in the kitchen, like I was a damn stray' (page 51) – he is made angry by his mother's insistence that he owes them a debt of gratitude. Recalling the Bible story of Lazarus and the rich man (Luke 16: 19–25), he says, with a conspicuous lack of charity, 'If it was a damn drop o' water I had to give them to save they life, they woulda dead' (page 51). Disagreement with his mother escalates to the edge of physical violence – he picks up a chair to hit her – and she is in doubt no longer: 'after your performance here today, raise yuh hand to kill yuh Ma, there is no power on God's earth could convince me say is not obeah that woman obeah you' (page 52).

Len's greatest malice is directed against George. In Luke 10: 30 a lawyer asks 'Who is my neighbour?' and Jesus answers with a parable. Len says to George 'We are neighbours' (page 34), but he does not wish him well. Len is no Good Samaritan like Lois's father (page 73). When George comes to ask for financial support, Len toys with him, and relishes his embarrassment (page 40). George thinks he has 'an enemy' (page 35): the enemy seems to be Len. Against the biblical injunctions,[14] he will render evil for evil. He can rationalise: 'McFarlane is vermin. I have a moral right to rid society of that sort of scum' (page 46). But he seems to be driven mainly by malice and the desire for revenge. When he has George cornered, he makes him squirm. 'Ten chances to one, you'll get buggered the first night in prison' (page 69). He coldly raises the possibility that George's wife and mother may also go to jail. 'Conspiracy to defraud. Jail again. It's going to be a full house!' No wonder George, kneeling, in a moment that recalls Len's schoolboy servitude (page 42), begs him 'Have a heart' (page 69). Len has been merciless. He is not in the business of overcoming evil with good.[15]

He is transformed at the end by the ritual retelling of the Cassava Nova incident in which his offer of love – for that is the burden of his grandiloquent letter (pages 70–71) – is cruelly rejected and the presumptuous 'lover-boy' is punished. Admonished, 'Don't forget' (page 72),[16] Len carries the hurt for years. He has been in thrall to bitterness since that traumatic night. He now is liberated into love. It is as though the humiliation of George, Miss Aggy's recognition of her appalling error, the selflessness displayed by Lois and by Pa Ben, combine to make forgiveness possible. Len's resentment has been exorcised. We have come to the end of the parable. Though Miss Aggy rushes at George to do him harm, the script allows him to escape. George and fair-skinned wickedness are now essentially irrelevant. The focus is on love and black community. As Pa Ben says: 'We bind ourselves together with strength and trust and confidence, and there was no doubt between us, no enmity in our hearts ...' (page 74).

Lois plays a crucial role in the movement towards love. When Len suspects Miss Aggy has set obeah in motion, Pa Ben advises: 'join hands with Miss Lois. She may have the solution to the problem.' He also implies that, unlike Len, she knows what obeah is. 'Is your roots and they grow deep! ... Miss Lois is roots, too. She'll understand. Depending on how much love, trust and understanding there is between you, the greater the chance you have of fighting this thing' (page 55). She and her father, a 'good Samaritan', took care of Len when he ran away from school (page 73). When, in the presence of

Miss Aggy, Pa Ben blurts out her name, he claims that what he said was 'Jesus Christ' (page 19). The choice is significant. For Lois's role is Christ-like at the end of the play. (In the first Jamaican production, directed by Rhone himself, Lois barred the door in an expansive gesture imaging the cross.) She follows Christ's injunction, 'Love your enemies, do good to them which hate you.'[17] Miss Aggy is now in danger from the boomerang of obeah set against Lois. Lois 'who is roots' understands the danger to Miss Aggy and to anyone who tries to counteract the process. Yet she bars the door and begins to say the twenty-third psalm. Miss Aggy, now repentant, pleads, 'No. No, don't do it. Don't endanger yourself. Pa Ben, warn her, tell her' (pages 73–74). But Lois has the solution. Knowing the risks, she continues to lead in the ritual. Pa Ben and Len join hands with her, and together they fight to save Miss Aggy. They are empowered by 'the one force that could counteract all evil': love (page 74).

Footnotes

1 Cf. Carl Stone: 'When I left high school in 1958, there were no persons of my complexion working in banks in non-menial positions as clerks, administrators, secretaries or managers. You had to have a light-coloured skin to hold those jobs.' *The Stone Columns: The Last Year's Work* edited by Rosemarie Stone (Kingston: Sangster's, 1994), page 100.

2 See Fernando Henriques, *Family and Colour in Jamaica* (London: MacGibbon and Kee, 1968; first published 1953; reprinted for Sangster's Book Stores, Kingston, 1976), particularly pages 50–70.

3 In a novel, *Stone Haven* (Kingston: Institute of Jamaica Publications, 1993), Evan Jones describes Munro in the late 1930s as 'a boarding establishment for ... boys, white, brown, and lately a black or two ...' (page 211).

4 'The brown man and the red man have always assumed social superiority over the blacks in every sphere of activity ...' Stone, page 96.

5 Again, the kingdom of heaven is like unto a merchant man, seeking goodly pearls: Who, when he had found one pearl of great price, went and sold all that he had, and bought it.' St Matthew 13: 45–6.

6 Lorraine Hansberry, *A Raisin in the Sun* (New York: Signet, 1988)

7 Errol John, *Moon on a Rainbow Shawl* (London: Faber, 1958)

8 Olive Senior, *Encyclopedia of Jamaican Heritage* (Kingston: Twin Guinep Publishers, 2003), page 355.

9 Leonard E. Barrett. *The Sun and the Drum*: African Roots in Jamaican Folk Culture (Kingston: Sangster's in association with Heinemann, 1976), page 25.

10 Senior, page 340.

11 'The period of mourning after death … ends with ceremonies on the ninth night, when it is believed the spirit of the dead finally departs.' Senior, page 352.

12 'And forgive us our trespasses, As we forgive them that trespass against us.'

13 *Good News Bible: The New Testament* (New York: American Bible Society, 1976), page 233.

14 Such as in Romans 12: 17, I Thessalonians 5: 15, and I Peter 3: 9.

15 'Be not overcome of evil, but overcome evil with good.' (Romans 12: 21).

16 The words 'don't forget' figured also in an earlier humiliation (page 46).

17 Luke 6: 27.

Performance And The Playwright's Craft

Presentation style

Rhone has achieved in *Old Story Time* a simple, flexible presentation style. Simplicity is emphasised in his notes on The Setting, Furniture and Costumes. The set he recommends is reversible, so that we can be shifted quickly from Miss Aggy's house to Len's (page 2). He has a similar approach to the furniture. 'With proper design and construction, the same piece of furniture serves as the bureau in MAMA's house, as well as the table in LEN's house/the Bank. Also, the coffee table covered with matting serves as the low bench in MAMA's house' (page 3). The note on Costumes helps the reader to visualise the characters; but its most important detail is the suggestion of 'a simple device' for marking off the flashbacks (page 4).

Rhone says he discovered the style in rehearsal:

> I said to the actors … 'I'm really not certain what the set should be, but I'm going to try something and let's see how it works.' I said: 'We will start with a bare stage, we will have no set. Whenever we absolutely need an object I will supply it. Come the end of Act I, whatever objects we have needed and used we will recycle for Act II'. It worked like an absolute dream. The absolute minimum, and really used and re-used. One can't do that with everything, but with that sort of play it was the perfect strategy to have adopted.[1]

In Rhone's Jamaican productions the transitions have been a theatrical marvel, cinematic in their easy flow, so the whole work seems – with Pa Ben dipping in and out, with journeys across space and time – one unbroken narrative, presented by Pa Ben. To introduce the housing scheme racket, for example, Pa Ben says, 'Suppose you want to start a housing scheme, you going to need money to borrow, so you go to George's bank' (page 43), and there before our eyes is George, the banker, using the telephone. Only minutes earlier we had seen him still in school, playing the overbearing bully.

That bullying sequence is very striking theatre. Pa Ben narrates, while the wickedness is elegantly mimed (pages 42–43). A few changes in position, some simple sound effects, an accessory or two, and a group of actors who have been a storyteller's audience suddenly become a buggy with horses arrogantly driven.

Mime is one of the storytelling methods. In the early scene when Len and Pearl are childhood friends, for example, they mime the journey to the river and jumping in. [*They race off, then freeze on the spot. When they break the freeze they are in the river, playing away, commenting on how cold the water is, accusing each other of wetting each other's hair, etc. MAMA appears behind them.*] (page 14). Audiences tend to be impressed by the theatrical economy. Another sequence that draws admiration is Pa Ben and Miss Aggy travelling back to town for the final scene. In Rhone's Jamaican productions their jiggling journey on the bus is mimed. 'In a flash we was heading back to town on the country bus "Surprise" (page 68).

Variations in language

Pa Ben narrates in Jamaican Creole, but the enactments introduce speech from various parts of the Jamaican language continuum. As Frederic Cassidy has pointed out, 'Jamaica Talk is not by any means of the same kind on all Jamaicans' lips.'[2] Pa Ben and Miss Aggy, of the same generation and living in the same rural community, sound broadly similar, but Miss Aggy's speech is strongly characterised by frequent appeals to the Lord, or Jesus, and references to the Bible. In those moments when Pa Ben is more the storyteller than a character in the story, there is often an element of self-conscious display in his language, as he projects his entertaining skill. He can be sharply critical. 'Sweet-mouth politician promise to bring down the moon, cut it up and hang it 'pon stick so we could read bible when night come. Ah boy, sixty years later, they don't even cut the stick yet' (page 7). He can even invent words for his purpose (in the speechifying tradition of the Jamaican tea-meeting): 'contuberance' and 'conbrucksion' are clearly ominous. 'Miss Margaret; Advancement; Advancement; till him gone like a fool write love-letter to the girl, and that's when the perpendicular meet the contuberance, which in lay the conbrucksion' (page 70).

Pearl and Len, when playing together in the village, sound very much like each other. 'Play bad when yuh mother not around. Is only because she gone to market why you manage to t'ief out.' 'I don't have to t'ief out.' (page 10). But Len's language is less relaxed when Miss Aggy calls him to account (page 11); and later, after education at Munro and in England, he is very formal and restrained. He is in conspicuous contrast with Pa Ben. 'Wo yoi! ... You 'member me?' 'How could I forget you, sir?' (page 21). Though his 'How many you have now?' moves towards Creole, the contrast with Pearl is also marked. 'How are you?' 'Me hearty.' 'And the children?' 'Them hearty too.' 'How many you have now?' 'Is eleven me gone' (page 22).

Lois speaks standard English habitually, often with an edge of sophistication, as in her quarrel with Len (pages 26–7), her early exchange with Miss Aggy (page 32) and her bemused response to Len's unusual display of affection in Act Two Scene Four (pages 65–6). George, most of the time, speaks a more casual English than Len and Lois which often includes constructions influenced by Creole. 'You have Tomlinson's phone number on you?' (page 4–6). Code switching[3] comes easily to him. 'Don't play the innocent with me' (Standard English) is immediately followed by 'Your mother-in-law tell me...' (Jamaican Creole for SE 'has told me'). 'I don't know what lie you cook up' (JC) runs into 'anyway I didn't come here to talk to you.' (SE) (page 63).

Activities

1   The Jamaican language continuum runs between Standard English (SE) and Jamaican Creole (JC) (sometimes called 'dialect' or 'patois'/*patwa*), with many variations in between.

    In the play, identify short passages of (a) Jamaican Creole; (b) Standard English; and (c) a mixture of JC and SE. In each instance, say which character is speaking. Speak each passage as if you were playing the role.

2   Translate into Standard English (a) a passage of Jamaican Creole; (b) a passage which mixes JC with SE. Read out your translations. Could they suitably replace the words in the play? If not, why not?

3   'Variations in language help to define the characters, their relationships and the situations they address.' Discuss.

4   Paying careful attention to the language used, act out pp. 20–22 (from Pa Ben's 'A year go by, and not a word. . .' to his 'When A come back, man. . . .') What does the language they use convey about the characters and their relationship to each other?

The storyteller(s)

The play was originally drafted without a storyteller. Rhone has explained that only when he hit upon the storytelling form did he solve the problem of how to present the whole forty-year span.[4] The playwright pretends Pa Ben, the main – but not the only – storyteller, is in control, determining emphases, omissions, the order of the information, 'the point of view'. He may allow us to see an episode played out in detail, or he may choose to move us swiftly across great tracts of time.

For example, after the sequence when Miss Aggy punishes Len, whom she finds playing with Pearl, Pa Ben says: 'The years went by, and the boy study him books, day and night, an' him pass all him exams with flying colours, yet still him couldn't get a job in the bank. But later for that. One day A happen to be in a next district about three miles from here, and A happen to see the boy with a pretty black girl' (page 12). (In 'later for that' he reminds us that, as storyteller, he can withhold information until he is ready to release it.) Similarly, Pa Ben compresses several years in a sentence when he says: 'Anyway as luck would have it, Missa Lenny never tarry too long on the dark continent. Two twos him was back in England, an' we gave thanks for his deliverance, an' there was no further cause for alarm or concern, till one evening …' (page 19).

The storyteller will sometimes comment on the action, trying to influence our responses. At the end of the play, for example, Pa Ben, while expressing his own feelings, is inviting us to cry. 'A tell you, every time A see the three of them together as a family, the feeling just well up inside, and the eye water… [He starts to cry in his joyfulness. He gets up, overcome with emotion, and goes towards his little house.] (page 74). The values Pa Ben projects are an important part of the story. At the beginning of Act Two, when he describes Len being bullied, he is most indignant. 'But is when they start to strut roun' like peacock, the fat slobs them dress up in they

Sunday go-to-meeting. Biggitty, oh so arrogant!' (page 42). Similarly, during the enactment of George's housing scheme racket, Pa Ben makes frequent editorial comment, such as 'Damn lie', and 'Greed married to ignorance' (page 45).

The interrelation between story and storyteller is not always as simple as that. There is a theatrically delightful moment, for example, when Pa Ben, having gone to get Miss Aggy, tells the story of his journey, which is also mimed on stage, at the same time as George, seated in Len's home, is reading through a dossier. 'Oh shit!' says George, reacting to the dossier. 'More or less,' adds Pa Ben, swiftly, interrupting the narrative of his journey (page 68). The manoeuvre vividly reminds us that Pa Ben is not only an active agent in one strand of the story, but is also the narrator of both strands.

The storyteller controls, of course, the order in which information becomes available, a fact to which attention is drawn at the beginning of Act Two. Pa Ben raises, through the proverb – "What sweet nanny goat." – "A go run him belly" (page 41) – the possibility that Len's triumphant laughter just before the intermission may be premature. He stimulates our curiosity and keeps us in suspense. 'Missa Lenny tell Miss Lois everything about the one Mongoose. … Well not quite everything. Him leave out a very important piece o' the story. … Not just what, but why' (page 41). That bit of information is kept from us until the final scene of the play. Similarly, after we have seen that George and Lois know each other (page 33), we are made to wait a while for details of their relationship (pages 64–66). The storyteller often directs our attention to the unanswered questions. When, for example, Pa Ben and Miss Aggy are travelling back into town for the final scene, Pa Ben reminds us that he does not know for certain whether Miss Aggy has set something in motion against Lois. 'The one question A wanted to ask Miss Aggy, A couldn't ask, but A had a feeling I would find out soon enough' (page 68).

Miss Aggy and George are also storytellers, in a sense. Miss Aggy 'tells' the story of how George persuaded her to pay down on a house (pages 29–31); George 'tells' how he blackmailed Lois at the bank (pages 64–66) and humiliated Len at school (pages 70–72). But in each of these cases the story being 'told' is enacted; and the storyteller disappears into the enactment. Pa Ben, on the other hand, at various stages literally tells parts of the story.

The beginning of the play establishes the storytelling atmosphere and the personality of the storyteller. After the darkness, the quiet folk song, the lantern glowing as he enters through the auditorium, Pa Ben enlists our involvement; for a storyteller depends on a responsive audience. He identifies himself as part of a tradition – his father was a storyteller – and begins to entertain us. The telling is a performance. He re-enacts his memory of 'stepping into the dance yard' and he does the pelvic gyrations of the 'corkscrew' dance. The storyteller may exaggerate: Pa Ben talks of reading by the light of fireflies in a bottle (page 7). He can and will invent: 'What A don't know as a fact, A will make up as A go along' (page 7), drinking some white rum if necessary.

The scene corresponds closely with the prototype of a traditional storytelling situation.

> The tale is acted out with body gestures, even when the storyteller is sitting. Sometimes he or she may stand up, move around, and mime parts of the action narrated. In most cases the public is not just watching. The public is active. It interacts with the teller, and the teller provokes this interaction by asking questions, welcoming exclamations, and turning to a song sung by all at appropriate points of the action. The teller and public are creating the tale together. The teller leads the event, but responds readily to the public and leads his or her public to experience the tale.[5]

Flashbacks

In a sense, the play is a series of flashbacks. If we take the present to be when Pa Ben says at the beginning, 'Evening, one and all' (page 6), then, as he tells the story, the enactments may be said to be flashbacks. But it is probably useful to recognise a difference between those enactments which illustrate the point in time Pa Ben's story has reached and those that go back further in time. We may therefore distinguish between the many flashbacks of Pa Ben, the main storyteller, and three which are introduced by others.

George, the villain, figures in each of these. He is a source of trouble to Miss Aggy, Lois and Len, in separate episodes. The second and third episodes are especially important, because they answer questions which have been raised, and highlighted, earlier in the story.

In the first episode, we see George persuading Miss Aggy to put money down on a house.

LEN: How did this Mister Mac encourage you?

MAMA: I was in the bank one day, the same bank A had the little savings in. [*LEN faces Up Stage and freezes. MAMA removes her hat, goes into her bag, takes out a red one and puts it on. GEORGE enters.*] (page 33)

Len's freeze signals the transition from Miss Aggy's telling in the present into the enactment of the encounter she has begun to tell us of. In his note on Costumes, Trevor Rhone suggests 'a simple device to help the flashbacks in the play, which is the use of red coloured accessories ...' (page 4). Red is a strong colour which remains strong in artificial light. It is also a colour which may have subliminal significance to Jamaicans; in Jamaican culture it is sometimes worn to keep the devil away.[7] When the action returns to the present (page 31), Len begins to move again and Miss Aggy changes her red hat.

In the second episode presented, George 'tells' how he manipulated Lois at the bank. Lois tells Len, ominously: 'George has something to tell you' (page 64). Then [*LEN moves Upstage and freezes. LOIS turns her back on the audience, puts on a jacket which suggests her bank uniform, then freezes ...*] When George is in position at the desk, he sends for her. In some productions the end of this flashback is stunningly effective. George has Lois cornered, having offered her the choice of either doing what he wants or being turned over to the police. He says, with menace, 'Come here.' She starts removing her jacket (a red accessory), takes tentative steps towards him; then, crying, runs away from him, out of the past into the present, the welcoming arms of Len (page 66).

Just before the final flashback, Len has required that, when Miss Aggy arrives, George tell her 'what happened that night ... and the events leading up to it' (page 69). After Miss Aggy enters, George says. 'Miss G.', and, puzzled, she enquires: 'What dis mean?' During Pa Ben's short anticipatory speech, George and Len go off. Miss Aggy and Lois stand with their backs to the audience, signalling another flashback.

The Cassava Nova flashback, enacting sexual humiliation, is intended to disturb the audience. Len passes through the auditorium screaming. It is as though he is screaming for generations of black people who have suffered similar oppression. '*In the darkness.*

LEN screams, terrible and long.' A spotlight picks him up, arriving through the auditorium, a pillow case over his head, his hands tied, his trousers about his ankles. This is a symbolic lynching, which Len has never forgotten.

Miss Aggy faces truth

Miss Aggy is appalled and angry, then contrite. She has been brought face to face with her misjudgement. The man she thought had been sent by God to guide her (page 31) is a 'wicked evil wretch!' (page 72). Much earlier Pa Ben had said, 'You have to face up to the truth'; had advised her, 'Examine yuhself' (page 20). She is doing this at last. She acknowledges her folly (echoing King Lear [6]): 'I am a foolish old woman' (page 73).

The placing of 'Cassava Nova'

The placing of the Cassava Nova incident so near the end is critical to the emotional and artistic effect of the play. It explains at last the origin of Len's obsessive malice against George. It reveals to Miss Aggy how mistaken she has been about George. It causes her also to recognise how mistaken she has been about Lois. Because Miss Aggy is at risk from forces she has wrongfully set in motion against Lois, her vulnerability provides an opportunity for the culminating ritual of love.

George having fled, and with Len emotionally transformed, Miss Aggy is enclosed in a saving circle.

George has fled. Len is now driven by love. Miss Aggy is encircled in the saving ritual.

A parable

The play is grounded in sociological accuracy. As a reader you may have questioned, however, whether it is just and credible at the end. Given his comprehensive villainy, can George be permitted to escape? Can Miss Aggy's lifelong attitudes be altered in a trice? Can Len so swiftly turn away from years of malice?

In the theatre they can. These questions are unlikely to occur to anyone witnessing a strong production. Audiences tend to be swept along, and to be moved by the closing moments: a flood of revelations and decisive action, Len's 'terrible' scream in the darkness, Miss Aggy's anger, the flight of George, Miss Aggy's contrition, the saving leadership of Lois, the ritual chant of the group, and ultimately *'silence as the circle is bathed with a warm rich light'* (page 74).

George has been defeated; he is punished by exposure and the loss of power. To pursue him further would be to prolong enmity, and Len has been distracted long enough. *Old Story Time* is a parable, primarily concerned to illustrate a moral or spiritual lesson. Pa Ben's parable extols the positive force of love.

1 Trevor Rhone interviewed by Mervyn Morris, *Jamaica Journal* Vol. 16 No. 1, February 1983, page 8.

2 Frederic G. Cassidy, *Jamaica Talk* (London: Institute of Jamaica and Macmillan, 1961; second edn 1971), page 2.

3 Trevor Rhone interviewed by Mervyn Morris, *Jamaica Journal*, page 8.

4 Jan Vansina, *Oral Tradition as History* (London: James Curry, 1985), page 34.

5 Madeline Kerr, *Personality and Conflict* in Jamaica (London: Collins and Sangster's, Jamaica, 1963), pages 122–3.

6 'I am a very foolish fond old man.' William Shakespeare, *King Lear* IV vii 60.

7 Again, the kingdom of heaven is like unto a merchant man, seeking goodly pearls: Who, when he had found one pearl of great price, went and sold all that he had, and bought it.' St Matthew 13: 45–6.

Questions about the play

1 Describe three of the means by which Pa Ben, as a storyteller, captures the audience's attention.

2 In *Old Story Time* suspense is created by withholding information the audience wants to have.

   (a) Identify two bits of information which the play withholds for a while.

   (b) Say why the information is important.

3 Describe two incidents from the play in which attitudes to colour are important.

4 There is frequent reference to the Bible in *Old Story Time*.

   (a) Identify three Bible references

   (b) Examine what each contributes to the play.

5 Describe Pa Ben's relationship to:

   (a) Miss Aggy
   (b) Lois
   (c) Len

6 Miss Aggy says, 'I only wanted what was best for him' (page 24).

   (a) What does Miss Aggy want for Len?
   (b) What does she do to get it for him?
   (c) Why is Len not grateful?

7 Describe Miss Aggy's personality and character, indicating what you consider to be her virtues and her defects.

8 Describe the role of each of the following and say what it contributes to the play:

   (a) Lois
   (b) Pearl
   (c) Margaret

9 Describe in detail George's relationship to two of the following:

   (a) Len
   (b) Lois
   (c) Miss Aggy

For general discussion

1 How relevant to your country today is the play's representation of attitudes to colour?

2 Should obeah be taken seriously?

3 What is love?

Exam-practice questions

1. Choose TWO of the following and show how Rhone makes use of them in developing the theme of identity:
   - Flashbacks
   - Characterisation
   - Costumes
   - Stage Directions.

   [25 marks]

2. Describe the roles of TWO of the following characters in *Old Story Time* and say why their roles are important:
   - Pearl
   - Lois
   - George
   - Len.

   [25 marks]

3. Pa Ben says, in the final scene of *Old Story Time*, "there was ... no enmity in our hearts, for we knew that the one force that could counteract all evil was there, and that force was love."

   (a) Choose TWO characters who show enmity. What reasons do they offer to justify the enmity?

   (15 marks)

   (b) How is the enmity transformed or defeated?

   (10 marks)

   [25 marks]

(Further Reading

Frederic G. Cassidy, *Jamaica Talk* (London: Institute of Jamaica and Macmillan, 1961; University of the West Indies Press, Kingston, 2007).

Pauline Christie, *Language in Jamaica* (Kingston: Arawak Publications, 2003).

Fernando Henriques, *Family and Colour in Jamaica* (London: MacGibbon and Kee, 1968; Sangster's Book Stores, Kingston, 1976), partic. pp. 50-70.

Errol Hill, 'The Emergence of a National Drama in the West Indies', *Caribbean Quarterly* Vol. 18 No. 4, December 1972, pp. 9-40.

Mervyn Morris, '*Is English We Speaking*' and other essays (Kingston: Ian Randle Publishers, 1999), 'Trevor Rhone: Three Plays', pp. 65-73.

Rex M. Nettleford, *Mirror Mirror: Identity, Race and Protest in Jamaica* (London and Kingston: Collins and Sangster, 1970; LMH Publishing Co., Kingston, 2000).

Trevor D. Rhone, *Bellas Gate Boy* (Oxford: Macmillan Caribbean, 2008).

Trevor D. Rhone, *Two Can Play and other plays* (Oxford: Macmillan Caribbean, 2008).

Trevor Rhone interviewed by Mervyn Morris, *Jamaica Journal* Vol. 16 No. 1, February 1983, pp. 3-13; reprinted in Mervyn Morris, *Making West Indian Literature* (Kingston: Ian Randle Publishers, 2005), 'Validating Lives: Trevor Rhone interviewed', pp. 65-74.

Olive Senior, *Encyclopedia of Jamaican Heritage* (Kingston: Twin Guinep Publishers, 2003).

Judy S. J. Stone, *Studies in West Indian Literature: Theatre* (London: Macmillan Caribbean 1994).)